INDOOR JUNGLE

THE *LEAF SUPPLY* GUIDE TO CREATING YOUR

INDOOR JUNGLE

Lauren Camilleri + Sophia Kaplan

Smith
Street
Books

CON-
TENTS

introduction

FROM INTERIOR WALLS COVERED in trailing Pothos to living-room corners overflowing with statement foliage, spaces really do come to life with the introduction of plants. Scrolling through Pinterest and Instagram and the seemingly endless photos of interiors filled to the brim with lush greenery may have you lusting after an indoor jungle of your very own. While inspiring, it's easy to be intimidated: how much time would it really take to care for all that greenery? Keeping ourselves alive can be a challenge, let alone having to keep thirty-plus plant babies thriving. The reality is, creating an urban jungle isn't just about filling your home with indoor plants – it's about adding the perfect amount of lushness to suit your space and lifestyle. Whether it's a single feature plant to greet you at your door or an apartment with more plants than furniture – there's a jungle solution for everyone.

Yes, plants are beautiful and we love them for the shape, texture and colour they add to a room, but they are so much more: they are enthralling and grounding, their presence promotes productivity, they can detoxify the air, and the act of caring for them and watching them thrive (or trying to nurse them back to health) is incredibly therapeutic. Clearly the advantages of keeping these leafy beauties goes far beyond just the aesthetic. Humans truly benefit from a connection to nature, particularly those of us living in densely populated cities with limited access to green space. Bringing plants into our homes and workplaces can be the perfect antidote to stress and anxiety, allowing us to take time to nurture these living things and, in turn, ourselves.

In our first book, *Leaf Supply*, we focused on how to introduce plants into your life, exploring some of the best foliage and succulent varieties to keep indoors and explaining how to keep them happy and healthy. This time around we're revisiting some of the important care info and taking a fresh view of some of the classic plants that can form the basis of your jungle. With *Indoor Jungle*, we're taking it up a notch by exploring some of the more interesting plants to add spice to your plant gang and showing how you can stylishly add greenery to beautify a space. With a greater

> An expansive warehouse in Melbourne is the perfect backdrop for a thoughfully edited collection of graphic statment plants (see more on page 186).

Whether your space is compact or vast, choosing the perfect varieties of plants and pairing each one with their ideal vessel means there's a potted plant (or twenty) to suit every space.

focus on plant styling, we go inside some of the most beautiful plant-filled homes, studios and public spaces around the globe (from the Netherlands to New York and from Byron Bay to Berlin) to see just how creative owners have cultivated their perfect indoor jungles.

From wild and overgrown (see the converted tram depot, Clapton Tram on page 124) to bold and minimal (such as the botanical apartment of a fashion designer in Berlin on page 132), there are myriad moods to create and endless ways in which plants can be introduced to incredible effect. The owners of these jungles offer great insight into how and why they have chosen to live with plants, and no doubt they will inspire you to find your own plant style.

We go room by room to see how plants can feature throughout your house in the most effective and practical ways. From the sanctuary of the bedroom to the gathering space of the living room, there's a way to introduce greenery to enhance functionality and add beauty. This time around, we touch on plant styling for balconies and courtyards, too. Particularly in apartment living, these spaces can become an extension of the interior and plants will help to seamlessly connect inside with out. These outdoor areas can provide the perfect conditions for many plants, complementing your indoor jungle and extending your enjoyment of these sometimes neglected spaces.

Whether your home is compact or vast, choosing the perfect varieties of plants and pairing each one with their ideal vessel means there's a potted plant (or twenty) to suit every space. We look at the importance of placing every plant in its optimum position, one that will provide them with the conditions they require to thrive. We need to remember that these living things have needs, such as light and water, and a healthy, happy plant will reward in the style stakes far more successfully than a dead and unhappy piece of foliage. Analysing your space really well before you go anywhere near a plant shop is a crucial step in creating an indoor jungle that will bring you many years of pleasure.

We hope the pages in this book will not only help you lay the groundwork for successfully bringing plants into your home or workplace, but will inform and inspire you to cultivate a plant style (and indoor jungle) that reflects your aesthetic and enhances your life.

‹ Bright light coming in through these large bedroom windows creates the ideal conditions for a collection of *Hoya* and *Rhipsalis*.

ATIONS

Schooling up and laying the correct groundwork for your indoor jungle is the best way to create a sustainable and ultimately rewarding plant-filled space. Knowing exactly what your plants need to survive, as well as what conditions they will receive in your interior, will allow you to make informed decisions about the style of jungle that is best suited to you.

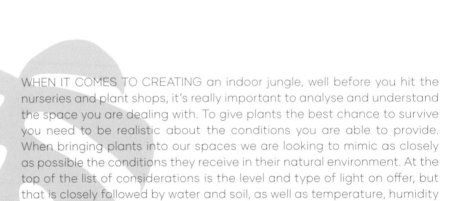

analysing your space

WHEN IT COMES TO CREATING an indoor jungle, well before you hit the nurseries and plant shops, it's really important to analyse and understand the space you are dealing with. To give plants the best chance to survive you need to be realistic about the conditions you are able to provide. When bringing plants into our spaces we are looking to mimic as closely as possible the conditions they receive in their natural environment. At the top of the list of considerations is the level and type of light on offer, but that is closely followed by water and soil, as well as temperature, humidity and fertiliser.

Spend some time throughout your day watching the sunlight as it moves through your home and peeks through different windows. Where does the light reach? Do certain rooms get extra hot in the afternoon sun? Do these patterns change in the cooler months? Do you have air conditioning or heaters? Or a strong draught down particular corridors? Keep all of this in mind when you're considering where to place your plants.

From here you can look more closely at which areas you would like to fill. Is there an empty corner that could be brought to life? A shelf or bookcase that could benefit from trailing plants? A windowsill that is screaming out for some plant love? Is there an ugly cabinet that could use covering up? A particularly beautiful little nook that you would like to draw the eye to with a delightful plant?

Now for the fun part; it's time to combine all these investigations and find the perfect plants for the perfect positions.

> Morning light streams through the large windows to the communal kitchen in Sydney's luxe co-working space La Porte Deux. A Fiddle leaf fig is perfectly positioned to enjoy the bright, indirect light.

getting inspired

THERE IS ABSOLUTELY NO SHORTAGE of places to find green inspiration when searching for ideas to create your own indoor jungle. We are stickybeaks from way back and love nothing more than peeking inside the spaces of amazingly creative plant people to swoon over how they have incorporated plants into their lives. From homes, studios and office spaces, to public areas and stores – we scoured the globe to find some of the most beautifully lush and inspiring places to include in the pages of this book. We gained invaluable insight chatting to the people who inhabit these verdant interiors, about how they've built their jungles, where their love of plants came from and, most importantly, why they love to live surrounded by them. Each jungle featured is unique in style and approach, showing that there are many different ways to bring plants inside. Here are some of the best places to get your greenspiration.

SOCIAL MEDIA Many of the spaces featured in this book belong to people we have long followed on Instagram. The visual feast contained within the millions of tiny squares on this platform is a constant source of inspiration for us. Follow plant people and hashtags, save and share images, and enjoy the unending supply of ideas and creative ways that people around the world are living with plants. Your first port of call: @leaf_supply – where it all began for us.

MAGAZINES, BOOKS + BLOGS The seemingly ever-increasing popularity of indoor plants means that when browsing the pages of interiors magazines, books and blogs you'll find plant-filled homes galore. From suggestions about pots and vessels for plants to beautiful indoor specimens in architecturally designed homes, these medias can offer awareness of different products and ideas, allowing you to visualise how you'll bring them into your own space.

‹ Plant inspiration can be found everywhere. This incredible Ponytail palm greets guests staying at the Paramount House Hotel in Sydney.

Displays in plant shops, such as the gorgeous Nikau Store in Byron Bay, give inspiration of how to incorporate plants into our own spaces. Nikki and Nicole stock a beautifully edited collection of lush plants, florals, botanical wares and art. Good luck leaving empty handed!

TRAVEL Venturing to new cities and countries is another amazing way of being exposed to incredible plant-filled spaces. Hunting down greenhouses at local botanical gardens when visiting a new city is one of our favourite things to do. These often historical and intricate buildings are packed with some of the world's most incredible plant species. The air inside the greenhouses is crisp and fresh and we challenge you to not come away with a number of new plants added to your lust list. In London, the Temperate House at Kew Gardens (the world's largest Victorian glasshouse) is filled with some of the rarest and most threatened species of plants on earth and is absolutely worth a visit. Hortus Botanicus in Amsterdam is another of the world's oldest greenhouses and is equally inspiring. In Paris, try the multiple Grandes Serres (large greenhouses) of the Jardin des Plantes; in New York, the sweet Enid A. Haupt Conservatory in the New York Botanical Garden; and in Sydney, the Latitude 23 Glasshouse at the Royal Botanic Gardens houses some incredibly rare plants, such as the White bat plant (*Tacca integrifolia*). Three other personal favourites can be found in the botanical gardens of Berlin, Palermo and Basel. If you don't have the ability to travel, see what gardens exist in your local neighbourhood. You might be surprised what you find.

Feeling adequately inspired? Perhaps you're feeling a little overwhelmed by the seemingly endless options and ideas you've found. It's time to start editing down and nutting out your ideas. Create a mood board (Pinterest is great for this or go old school and make one IRL) with some of your favourite plants, pots and those images that really capture what you want to cultivate. Refer back to this regularly to make sure you're staying on track, but also don't feel that you are married to your initial ideas. It is absolutely fine for your vision and style to evolve as you begin to cultivate your indoor jungle.

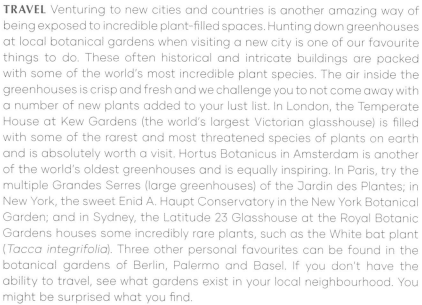

PLANT CARE

When it comes to plant care information and advice, many people are looking for specific rules to follow to ensure they are doing exactly the right thing to help keep their plants alive. There is an assumption that if you water a certain number of times a week or give a plant the exact light you think it requires then it should look perfect at all times. While understandable, this simplified approach to plant care can create unrealistic expectations about these living and complex beings, and can lead to disappointment and a sense of failure when things don't go according to plan. It also assumes that the appreciation of houseplants lies purely in the aesthetic, that yellowing older foliage or an unusual growth pattern is unattractive and annoying rather than part of the plant's natural aging process or a quirk to be admired and celebrated.

A large part of the joy of maintaining an indoor jungle is obtained through the process of tending to and nurturing the plants. Really observing and understanding your plants' needs will allow you to appreciate the experimental side of indoor gardening and to gain confidence in being able to adapt your care to their changing requirements.

In this section, we will explore the fundamentals of plant care and try to give you a greater understanding of how each of the elements work together to create the ideal growing situation for your plant babies. While our easy-to-understand key provides a really general guide to caring for some of the species we profile, with your greater understanding of the basics – the main ones being light, water and soil – we hope to equip you with a more integrated approach to plant care. Providing the ideal environment, observing and getting to know your plants in more detail, and understanding and accepting the way they adapt to their new home is the most comprehensive way to undertake plant parenthood. It will also leave you better able to tailor your care to suit your plants' specific needs and to troubleshoot effectively when necessary.

light

THIS IS WITHOUT A DOUBT the most important place to start when it comes to talking about plant health as, above all else, plants need light to survive. Light is integral to the process of photosynthesis, in which plants create their own fuel by utilising a combination of carbon dioxide and water and using light energy to convert it into glucose and oxygen.

Many of the plants that do well indoors hail from the tropics where they have adapted to growth in rainforests with dappled light, shaded by the tree canopy above. The term bright, indirect light is used to best describe this light situation but is fairly broad (read: vague) and can leave many new plant parents in the dark. This outdoor 'shaded' position protects the foliage from harsh direct sun in their natural environment but is generally far brighter than even the brightest spot indoors. Working out the quantity and quality of light in your space is incredibly important and while it takes some analysis and experimentation, your plants will thank you for it.

Start by identifying the light sources in your space. Most likely these will be vertical windows and doors but if you're really lucky, you may have a skylight or two that will provide some seriously good and consistent light for plants. It will also be important to assess how the light levels change in your space over the course of the day and from season to season. It's time to start thinking like a plant. It sounds a little kooky, but getting down to the level of your plants and seeing what they see is very useful.

It makes sense that the closer you get to the light sources in your space, the brighter the light. A sunny windowsill will provide the most intense light and will be best suited to sun-worshipping Cacti and Succulents. Direct sun coming in through a window may be too intense for some indoor foliage, so placement close to, but not directly exposed to, the rays is best. These plants will generally see the sky uninterrupted for most of the day which should provide plenty of bright, indirect light to help them thrive. The further you get from a light source, the lower the quality and quantity of the light becomes. Plants sitting on the opposite side of the room to the light source with no direct view to the sky will generally experience what we would consider 'low light' conditions.

To make a more accurate assessment of the light, a light meter is the tool you're looking for. Physical light meters can be quite expensive, so instead we recommend trying a light meter app which you can download straight to your smartphone and will suffice for most indoor gardeners. An even cheaper method is the shadow test, which requires nothing more than a piece of paper. On a sunny day place the piece of paper in the spot you would like to position your plant. Hold your hand around 30 cm (12 in) above the paper to reveal a shadow. A dark, clearly defined shadow with clean edges suggests bright light. If you can see a lighter, fuzzier shadow where you can still make out the shape of your hand, this would be medium light. If the shape of the hand is very poorly defined, you're looking at a low light situation.

> A thriving *Begonia* soaking up some gorgeous dappled light in the Amsterdam home of photographer Janneke Luursema (see more on page 196).

As mentioned, the light will change throughout the course of a day and as the seasons change. In winter and autumn, the sun sits lower in the sky and plants that were receiving adequate light in summer and spring can start to suffer. Be sure to stay on top of this changing light situation and adjust the position of your plants throughout the year. You may need to shift certain plants closer to light sources or sit them higher up on furniture or plant stands.

It can be quite disheartening to discover that your space is not as adequate for sustaining indoor plant life as you may have hoped. In these instances, grow lights can make a significant difference. The use of full spectrum LED lights, which produce a balance of cool and warm light replicating the natural solar spectrum, will allow you to successfully grow indoor plants in those darker spots. There's a range of lights and systems on the market but you can start by introducing some individual grow light bulbs in ordinary light fittings without the need for a full hydroponic set-up.

Many of the plants that do well indoors hail from the tropics where they have adapted to growth in rainforests with dappled light, shaded by the tree canopy above.

water

ALONG WITH LIGHT, plants need water to survive and indoors they rely on us to appropriately meet their liquid needs. It is probably the area of plant maintenance that confuses and stresses new plant parents the most; no doubt you've heard how many plants have met an untimely death due to overwatering. However, with a greater understanding of the role water plays in sustaining plants, as well as the factors that can affect the rate at which a plant absorbs water, you will be better placed to water more effectively and avoid some of the pitfalls of over and underwatering your plant babies.

When an indoor plant is receiving the right amount of light and is potted in a mix that is adequately aerated, it will absorb water through its roots effectively, delivering nutrients and minerals to where they are needed most and filling out plant cells (along with cellulose) providing good structural support for stems and foliage. Overwatering essentially drowns your plant, as it stops oxygen from being able to reach the roots and puts your plant at risk of root rot (while underwatering will slowly starve your plant of the moisture and minerals it requires). When watering is inadequate a plant will often communicate distress either by dropping leaves or presenting with browning or yellowing foliage.

All plants require different levels of watering. It's impossible to say that a specific plant needs to be watered once a week or once a fortnight, as there are so many different variables. How big is the pot the plant sits in? A larger pot will generally dry out less quickly. Is the pot exposed to heat sources such as direct sunlight? Is it a little close to a heater, which will dry out the soil faster? Is the pot placed among a group of other plants? This proximity will increase humidity and keep your plant's soil moist for longer.

The absolute best way to test the moisture level of your plant's soil is to simply press your finger a few inches into the soil and feel how much has dried out. Do this every few days until you begin to understand its needs. Most (not all) tropical indoor plants like the first couple of centimetres (an inch or so) of soil to have dried out before watering again. Always check the specific water requirements your plant needs, and then be sure to adjust them according to the seasons (ie. water less often in winter when the soil is likely to dry out more slowly and plants tend to go through more dormant growing periods).

If you're not feeling super confident about your moisture-sensing abilities or have plants in awkward-to-reach places, a water meter will be your friend. Simply insert the prong into the soil and it will give you a clear reading of moisture levels, which you can then use to decide whether your plant is ready to water again.

When you are ready to water, give your plants a good soak. Ideally, all pots should have drainage holes and you want to provide enough water so that it runs freely out of the base of the pot each time. Empty the saucer about half an hour after you have watered to ensure the plant isn't sitting in stagnant water. Lukewarm water is best – too cold and it can shock your plant. Re-filling your watering can after you've finished watering means the next time you go to water you will have room-temperature water that has also had time to purify. Letting your tap water sit out for at least 24 hours allows chlorine and other harmful minerals to dissipate and makes it more friendly for your sensitive friends, such as Calathea and palms.

If you really want to treat your indoor plants, getting them outside when it's raining – or even collecting rainwater to water with inside – will give them a beautiful boost. This liquid gold is what they're used to drinking in the wild and is free from the chemicals and minerals found in our tap water that can build up in the soil. If you do take plants out to water, just be sure to bring them inside before it gets too cold or too hot. Sudden drops in temperature and direct sun on precious foliage can cause irreversible damage in a fairly short amount of time.

Jamie Song waters his Chinese money plant with a teapot. The narrow nozzle allows for accurate water delivery.

soil

GOOD-QUALITY, WELL-SUITED potting mix is a crucial foundation that will nurture strong, healthy growth in your indoor jungle. Use the wrong potting mix, and you'll find that despite your best efforts when it comes to placement and watering, your plants will struggle to thrive.

There are four key elements to consider when it comes to potting mix: levels of moisture retention, aeration, drainage and nutrients. Potting mix is a combination of different ingredients which fulfil these requirements in different ways. Many of the more advanced indoor growers out there prefer to make up their own potting mix, customising ingredient ratios to suit specific plants. While this isn't totally necessary, there is something fun about getting your hands dirty mixing ingredients and is actually easier than it sounds because most tropical indoor plants require a very similar mix.

That said, it is perfectly acceptable to buy potting mix from your local hardware or gardening store. Be sure to select the highest-quality organic indoor potting mix. Store-bought potting mix generally has enough nutrients to support happy growth for about six to twelve months. After which point you'll need to start adding your own fertiliser (more on that in the following chapter).

Whether you use store-bought or make your own, you want your soil to be open, loose and nutrient rich. Play around with ratios, but generally for tropical plants you want a base of approximately 60 per cent of moisture-retaining material, 30 per cent aerating and draining material, and the final 10 per cent covering off nutrients. You'll need a greater portion of aerating and draining material for Succulents and Cacti as they prefer far less moist environments.

The term 'soil' can be a bit of a misnomer when it comes to indoor plants. Potting mixes are often soilless, so we'll break down some of the most common components used for growing mediums to demystify the dirt, in order to help you select, or mix, the best potting mix for your plant needs.

MOISTURE RETENTION

The base of most indoor potting mixes consists of moisture-retaining material that is also generally well aerated and well draining. Potting mix needs to be able to absorb water to allow for moisture and nutrients to enter the plant system via its roots.

Peat moss Although a very popular product, the current rate of peat moss harvesting is unsustainable and contributing to long-term environmental damage. We highly recommend trying one of the two following materials.

Coir peat Also known as coconut coir, this is a great alternative to peat moss as it's a sustainable by-product of the coconut industry. Coir peat is a stable growing medium that is both lightweight and able to hold water well, and for this it is our go-to.

Homemade compost If you have the outdoor space, making your own compost is a brilliant way to reduce your own waste and give back to the environment. Properly decomposed compost is not only water retaining but a nutrient-dense treat for your plants.

AERATION + DRAINAGE

Roots need to be able to take up oxygen and can only do so if there is adequate aeration in the potting mix. In nature, worms and other creatures help to ensure soil stays light and loose, but indoors, and with the added impact of overhead watering, soil can become compacted. To avoid this, it is essential that potting mix contains one of the following materials.

Vermiculite A mined mineral that expands into light brown particles when heated. It adds magnesium and calcium and has greater water-holding capacity than perlite.

Perlite A mined volcanic rock that expands when heated. It's a sterile material that's bigger than vermiculite and looks a bit like styrofoam.

Pumice Another volcanic rock and our personal pick. It's a bit heavier than perlite, meaning that it doesn't float to the top of your mix and fly away, but still offers the same aerating qualities. The pores of pumice also help store and slowly release nutrients and water.

Sand This is super beneficial when it comes to drainage and helps to mimic the desert-like environs of Succulents and Cacti.

NUTRIENTS

Plants need nutrients to thrive. Most plants require fertilising every so often but ensuring there is some in your potting mix to begin with means your plants are given a kick start in life.

Worm castings This is effectively worm poop and is an incredibly rich source of nutrients for your plants.

Recycled mushroom compost This is the compost mushrooms are grown in, which is then recycled once the mushrooms have finished cropping. It improves soil structure and releases nutrients slowly.

Fish emulsion Made up from what would otherwise be unused fish parts this is a gentle but still effective nutrient addition.

plant hack

Making your own potting mix allows to you create something that is customised to your needs (while still being suitable for your plants). A combination that supports greater moisture retention can help if you're a little forgetful when it comes to watering, or blend a well-draining mix if you're more of an overzealous waterer.

some other considerations

YOU'VE GOT LIGHT, WATER AND SOIL sorted, so now there are a few other things to keep in mind while you're creating the perfect home for your plant friends.

TEMPERATURE In some senses, indoor plants are much more protected than their outdoor peers. They won't suffer from the damages of frost or hail but they are at the mercy of your heaters and air-conditioning units. Most indoor plants hail from tropical or subtropical climes and, as a general rule, prefer a daytime temperature of 15–24°C (60–75°F) with a drop of a few degrees overnight (3–5°C/5–10°F), which mimics its natural environment. Indoor plants will tolerate occasional summertime highs of up to 32°C (90°F), but will get stressed staying at this temperature for too long so do your best to lower the degrees during heatwaves and keep plants clear of heaters.

HUMIDITY Most tropical plants like things a little steamy. Air conditioning and dry air can really zap the moisture from your plants, so it's important to keep tabs on the moisture levels in the air. While Succulents and Cacti can deal with much drier conditions both above and below the surface, tropical plants' ideal situation is a relative humidity of 50 per cent. If it drops below 30 per cent, a plant's roots will struggle to absorb an adequate amount of water to keep up with the moisture loss through the leaves.

Grouping your plants together creates a microclimate that helps to boost humidity levels and makes misting all their leaves a cinch! Regular misting is a must for many tropical plants but is a relatively short-lived (and labour-intensive) solution. For something more longstanding, try using humidity trays where you place your plants on pebble- and water-filled saucers (the pebbles ensure the base of the pot isn't actually touching the water). If you're really getting desperate you can buy a humidifier which will have the added benefit of keeping your skin from drying out as well!

FERTILISER Plants in the wild have constant access to fresh nutrients, through composting plant matter and treats left by passing animals and insects. Indoors, a premium potting mix should contain enough fertiliser to keep your plants happy for about six months. But after this point you'll need to give your plants a helping hand. There are three main nutrients found in most fertilisers: nitrogen for chlorophyll and plant protein production, phosphorus for healthy root systems and potassium for disease resistance.

Generally, tropical indoor plants like to be fertilised every one to three months during the warmer growing periods. When things get a little quieter in winter, be sure to give your plant a rest. We use an organic liquid fertiliser and dilute it twice as much as suggested on the bottle so as to avoid scorching the delicate roots of our plants. It's always worth checking the specifics of each plant as some, such as pitcher plants or Staghorn and Elkhorn ferns, don't require much in the way of additional nutrients and probably only need a diluted fertiliser boost once a year.

> Moisture-loving plants are great for bathrooms. Hardier ferns, such as Elkhorns, are well equipped to withstand the high temperatures from steamy showers.

THE PLANTS

Fabulous foliage is what it's all about. From ubiquitous favourites like Devil's ivy and the Swiss cheese plant to the rarer beauty of the Purple shamrock and Mini monstera, we profile the plants that will make your indoor jungle sing. Get to know your plant pals a little more intimately with some individual care info and our tips on how to best style them in your space.

Plant care key

light care

Be aware that light conditions will vary from season to season. Reposition plants accordingly to ensure that their light needs are consistently being met.

Low–moderate Tolerant of shady conditions, but will thrive in bright, indirect light.
Bright, indirect Enjoys a position that receives diffuse bright light; avoid direct sunlight.
Bright, direct Enjoys bright light and will tolerate and appreciate some direct sun.

water care

Dipping your finger into the top layer of soil is the best way to monitor the watering needs of your plants. Note that seasonal differences will affect watering frequency, and you will generally need to reduce watering in the cooler months.

Low Water roughly once a fortnight or when the majority of the soil has dried out.
Moderate Water roughly once a week when the first 5 cm (2 in) of soil has dried out.
High Water roughly twice a week when the soil surface has dried out.
Misting Spritz your plant leaves using a spray bottle filled with water once a week or so, to increase humidity levels.

soil care

Where possible, use top-quality organic potting mix specifically formulated for individual plant types.

Well-draining Water is able to drain easily with the addition of vermiculite or perlite, which increases aeration while retaining valuable nutrients.
Moisture-retaining A potting mix that retains moisture with the inclusion of peat or compost.
Coarse + sandy A potting mix with a high content of sand and grit, which allows water to quickly drain away from the roots – perfect for desert dwellers.

the classics

The stalwarts, the stayers, the enduring favourites. These are the indoor plants that can form the basis of your indoor jungle. Generally easy to source, care for and beautifully adapted to interior conditions, we like to think of them as the sure-fire hits in any space.

THE PLANTS

Swiss cheese plant
Monstera deliciosa

LIGHT
Bright, indirect

WATER
Moderate +
misting

SOIL
Well-draining

style note

• These beauties are incredibly versatile and can work in numerous styling situations. Larger specimens look amazing as standalone feature plants, while smaller plants pair beautifully with other tropicals, such as this Devil's ivy in a hanging pot, to create some serious jungle vibes.

A plant that really needs no introduction, the Monstera is an enduring favourite on the houseplant scene and despite its ubiquity, it will always be at the top of our list. Hailing from southern Mexico through to southern Panama, it is the large, graphic fenestrations of its foliage, along with an easy-going nature, that makes it an awesome addition to any space.

Broken down, the Latin name *Monstera deliciosa* refers to the 'monstrous' size this plant can grow to under the right conditions, as well as the 'delicious' fruit it bears. Although unlikely to flower or fruit indoors, in the wild, the fruit, resembling a green corn cob, is quite the spectacle. Said to taste like fruit salad, it is the inspiration behind one of the plant's many common names. We also love the French name for the Monstera – plante gruyère – which refers to the Swiss cheese-like holes in the leaves, as well as the Sicilian name – zampa di leone – which means lion's paw.

Monsteras require room to thrive. While their indoor growth is likely to be significantly less than the 20 metre (60 ft) height they can reach in the wild, in favourable indoor conditions they can be prolific growers. In the jungle, aerial roots allow these monsters to clamber up existing trees towards the light. To help maintain upright growth indoors it can be helpful to support the plant by staking. Or if it's sitting in a higher position let it naturally splay down and outwards.

When it comes to care, the Monstera really shines as it is delightfully low maintenance. A weekly soaking usually does the trick: water deeply, allowing any excess to drain away from the roots. Occasional misting can help create the tropical environment you're trying to mimic. Wilting or yellow leaves are generally a sign of overwatering. If this happens, remove any dead or damaged leaves and reduce watering to allow the plant to recuperate. As with all large-leaved plants, it's good practice to clean the leaves with a damp cloth or pop it in the shower to regularly remove dust. Fertilise monthly in the warmer seasons, and re-pot once you notice it becoming root-bound. You'll know that your plant is root-bound if you see roots peeking out the drainage holes or if your plant seems listless with stunted growth and browning or yellowing leaves.

LIGHT
Bright, indirect

WATER
Moderate +
misting

SOIL
Well-draining

Sabre fig
Ficus maclellandii 'Alii'

Although certainly one of the lesser-known members of the Ficus family, the Sabre fig deserves no less love than its more popular relatives, the Fiddle leaf fig (*Ficus lyrata*) and the Rubber plant (*Ficus elastica*). With beautifully elegant proportions, the Sabre fig is tall and dainty with thin and pointy dark-olive leaves reminiscent of some Australian natives.

They're relatively slow growers, but look beautiful at any size. If you want to make a real impression, opt for a mature specimen. To encourage growth, we recommend re-potting every two years at the end of winter, but be sure to increase your pot size gradually as too large a leap will shock your plant or allow the soil to become waterlogged.

Sabre figs enjoy bright, indirect light, but will tolerate slightly lower-light conditions as well. Regular rotation of the plant will ensure even growth as their branches reach out towards the light source.

Unlike other members of the fig family, the Sabre fig doesn't have a tendency to drop leaves (unless over-watered) and is relatively pest and disease resistant. One thing to note is to keep curious little hands and paws at bay, as the sap is mildly toxic and can irritate the skin.

To keep your Sabre fig looking its best, fertilise with liquid fertiliser once a month in the warmer months.

style note

- Large specimens of the Sabre fig make particularly effective indoor trees and look incredible in minimal concrete pots, helping to fill empty corner spaces or taking centre stage in an entrance or hallway.

Variegated rubber plant
Ficus elastica 'Tineke'

While we love a Rubber plant as much as any other, when you're looking for something a little more, shall we say, flamboyant, then look no further than the Tineke, or variegated Rubber plant. You get all the positives of this reliable classic, but with some added pizzazz. Sporting mottled cream, green and blush-coloured glossy leaves, it's a real eye-catcher either sitting alone or adding colour to a group of green plants.

To maintain that glorious patterning on the foliage, the Tineke needs a little more light than its non-variegated cousins, but that aside it's just as easy to care for. If the variegation begins to fade or it starts to drop its lower leaves, be sure to pop it in a brighter position. Falling leaves could also be a sign of overwatering.

The Tineke will communicate its thirst by wilting, but avoid getting to this point by implementing a regular watering schedule. A good soak roughly once a week should do the trick, but as long as the top few centimetres (inches) of soil have dried out, you are good to water again. Those wide, robust leaves are real dust-catchers, so wipe them down regularly with a damp cloth. A spray of white oil will also keep the leaves super glossy with the added benefit of keeping pests at bay. Avoid hot and cold draughts, as they can be sensitive to drastic changes in temperature. The sap is mildly toxic, so keep clear of pesky pets and curious little ones.

Rubber plants are one of the best plants for increasing air quality and are also pretty resistant to pests and disease. Other unusual varieties worth checking out include the darker variegated Ruby and super-moody Black prince.

style note

• With a tree-like stature and propensity to grow big, Tinekes are generally best placed on the floor. A lower position is also important for enjoying its beautiful foliage from above. Pair with a minimal pot – think cylinder- or egg-shaped – so as not to distract from the glorious patterning on the leaves.

LIGHT
Bright, indirect

WATER
Moderate

SOIL
Well-draining

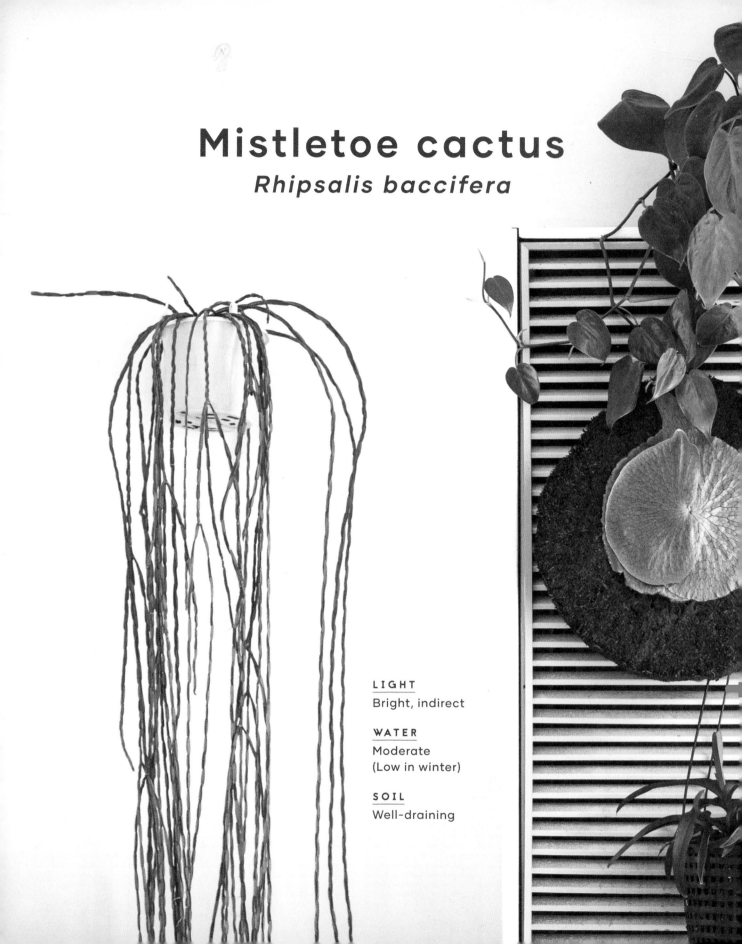

Mistletoe cactus
Rhipsalis baccifera

LIGHT
Bright, indirect

WATER
Moderate
(Low in winter)

SOIL
Well-draining

Another gorgeous and textural jungle dweller, the Mistletoe cactus hails from the rainforests of South and Central America and can also be found across Africa and Sri Lanka. There are many varieties of *Rhipsalis*, but the mistletoe is particularly dramatic with its mass of thin stems that cascade beautifully over the edges of its pot. It is the delicate white flowers that are followed by white berries, similar to that of traditional mistletoe, which gives the plant its common name.

Like the Fern leaf cactus (see page 54), the Mistletoe is a jungle cactus that does not do well in desert-like conditions. It can handle a small amount of direct morning or late afternoon sun, but anything more will burn the stems. Its love of humidity means a well-lit bathroom is ideal – just ensure that the soil dries out between watering to avoid root rot, and cut back substantially during the colder months. Clay pots work really well as they allow the soil to breathe, helping to dissipate moisture. Pots can also be suspended from a leather or rope macrame hanger.

LIGHT
Bright, indirect

WATER
Moderate

SOIL
Well-draining

Bird of paradise
Strelitzia

There are some plants whose mere presence can transport you to warmer climes. The Bird of paradise, with its large paddle-shaped leaves hailing from the coastal forests of South Africa, is one such plant. We often talk about statement plants and there is no denying that when it comes to the *Strelitzia* that statement is, 'we are in the tropics!' Although there are five varieties of *Strelitzia*, only two are readily grown indoors: the *Strelitzia reginae* with its brilliant orange flowers and the *Strelitzia nicolai*, which has vivid white flowers and a black 'beak'.

In all honesty though, it's unusual for either to flower indoors, so choosing between the two usually comes down to foliage preference and space. The *Strelitzia nicolai* has greener, shinier, longer and broader leaves, and it can get seriously big (it can grow to 9 metres/30 ft tall in the wild). The *Strelitzia reginae*, on the other hand, has greyer leaves that are proportionally narrower, a little heavier and more stiff than the Nicolai. Once the Reginae reaches about 1.5 metres (5 ft) tall it starts growing horizontally, forming offsets.

Both varieties can grow relatively fast in the right conditions and thus need plenty of room to really shine. *Strelitzia* like a lot of bright light, some direct sun and for the soil to be kept moist, but not water-logged, and warm (this tropical babe is not especially tolerant of the cold). Another thing to consider is that strong wind in a balcony position or regularly brushing past the leaves in, say, an entrance or hallway can cause it to shred. To keep the foliage looking fabulous, consider placing the plant somewhere sheltered and free from foot traffic!

Occasional browning or yellowing leaves can be cut off close to the soil surface. If the leaves become brown and crunchy, you are probably over-watering, and if the leaves furthest from the centre start yellowing, you are under-watering. To flower, *Strelitzia* need to be four to five years' old, root bound and given some outdoor time, shielded from direct midday sun. It will become a heavy pot to move around, but worth it for those beautiful blooms.

style note

• If it's tropical vibes you're after, there really is no substitute for the *Strelitzia*. Let that foliage do the talking in a simple white or concrete lightweight planter that's big enough to contain this impressive beauty, yet light enough to transport it if necessary.

Devil's ivy
Epipremnum aureum

LIGHT
Bright, indirect

WATER
Moderate

SOIL
Well-draining

Truly one of the easiest indoor plants to grow, Devil's ivy (also known as Pothos) is a fast and furious type that's also top-notch for improving air quality in your space. This tropical vine really is a winner indoors, because it can be trained to grow in any direction and gets lush seriously quickly. Available in a variety of cultivars, from the common gold and green variegated Golden pothos to the light-green Neon pothos and the stylish white and green-speckled Marble queen, there's bound to be one that tickles your fancy.

They look lovely draping down over shelves or you can use hooks to train them up walls or around door frames. They do have small aerial roots that can attach to trees or walls, but some assistance is usually required inside to get them to cling where you want. They can grow to an astounding 20 metres (66 ft) tall, and without much effort they'll begin to takeover your space (in the best possible way, of course), but they are equally easy to tame and keep in check with regular pruning.

style notes

• Trailing these lush beauties from a bookshelf or plant stand is a no-brainer, but to create a real impact, train it up and across a wall to really jungle it up.

• Another creative way to display Devil's ivy is to set up a stylish propagating station with a variety of glass vessels filled with a multitude of cuttings. Just be sure to change the water regularly to maintain the health of the cuttings.

care note

• Older leaves will yellow as part of the normal aging process of the plant. Be sure to regularly prune old leaves so the plant can focus its energy on producing fresh new growth.

In good news for those of us with a propensity for neglect, Devil's ivy is beautifully resilient and forgiving. Although they will do best in bright, indirect light, they can absolutely tolerate lower-light conditions. Just note that the water requirements will decrease in a reduced light situation. It's good practice to re-pot every couple of years even if the growth seems to be slowing down.

They are also super easy to propagate: simply take a stem cutting of at least 10 cm (4 in) from below a leaf node and place it in water. Top up the water every week if it continues to looks clean or replace with fresh water if it starts to look a little murky. Give it a few weeks to develop a root system and then plant it back in its original pot to thicken up the original plant or create a new plant all together. It's a super cheap way to build your jungle and a lovely gift for friends and family.

Fern leaf cactus
Selenicereus chrysocardium

OK, so technically the Fern leaf cactus is not a foliage plant, but this prehistoric-looking epiphyte with bold, jagged 'leaves' looks so good in an indoor jungle environment that we just had to include it! If its graphic, flattened stems aren't enough of a selling point, then the kicker is in its equally gorgeous flower, a delicate and fleeting beauty. The flower has wonderful golden stamens in its centre, and although this plant will flower during the day, many Chrysocardiums only flower at night, by the light of the moon – dreamy!

You would be forgiven for being slightly confused by this succulent's common name. While 'fern leaf' refers to the shape of the stems, it's a rather unusual looking 'cactus'. It is in fact a jungle cactus that has evolved from a drought-tolerant desert-dweller to adapt to the humid, shadier climes of the jungle. When this species moved to the tropics, moisture retention was no longer an issue and instead finding the light became more important, so it spread its leafless stems wide to aid the photosynthesis process.

Native to Mexico, the Fern leaf cactus is generally pretty easy to care for. Unlike desert Cacti, direct sun is a no-no, so keep the light bright but indirect. Water when the top layer of soil is dry; this will generally be less often during the cooler months.

LIGHT
Bright, indirect

WATER
Moderate
(Low in winter)

SOIL
Well-draining

style note

• Whether it's placed in
the bathroom, bedroom
or living room, the Fern
leaf cactus looks incredible
trailing from a high shelf
with those zig-zag leaves
popping off a white wall.
Pair it with Mistletoe
cactus (see page 44) and
Devil's ivy (see page 50)
to mix up the textures
and create a curtain
of trailing greenery.

Wax plant
Hoya

LIGHT
Bright, indirect

WATER
Low + misting

SOIL
Well-draining

style note

• Hoyas are best left in the spot they first find their home, so be thoughtful in their placement. We recommend placing them somewhere bright, so you don't miss out on their beautiful blooms.

While many indoor plants are selected for their foliage alone, there are instances where the flowers of a plant are equally spectacular. The thick, waxy leaves of the *Hoya* are available in an incredible variety of shapes, sizes, colours and textures, but it is the stunning clusters of sweet-scented, star-shaped flowers that make these plants truly special.

A tropical plant native to Australia and East Asia, Wax plants are perfect for trailing from a hanging basket or trained up a support. Due to the robustness of their succulent leaves, they are tough little plants that will continue to grow without too much fuss and enjoy being left to dry out between waterings.

Indoor Hoyas need to be fully mature before they will flower and even then only with the right care. So what is right, in *Hoya* terms? It is mostly to do with light and the best way to encourage the plant to flower is to place it in extremely bright light, but not full sun. Water deeply when it's warm, then ease off substantially in winter.

Because most Hoyas are epiphytic, they like to be root-bound. If re-potting, do so in a pot that's only slightly bigger than the one you're moving it from. It will enjoy, but doesn't demand, a feed in summer of half-strength liquid fertiliser once every two weeks. The best time to do this is last thing at night just before you turn out the lights, or in the morning when the air is cool.

Begonias

LIGHT
Bright, indirect

WATER
Low–moderate

SOIL
Well-draining

Begonias were probably much-loved by your grandma, but don't be fooled into thinking they're only for old folk to appreciate. With some of the most stunningly decorative foliage in the indoor plant world, this vibrant and prolific group of plants can add some serious interest to your jungle. There are over 1800 species of *Begonia*. Among our favourites are the spotted wings of the *Begonia maculata*, the round green umbrella leaves of the *Begonia acida* and the delicate white flowers of the *Begonia solananthera*.

Because they enjoy humidity, but don't like having wet leaves, it's best to grow Begonias with other humidity-loving plants where they will create their own little greenhouse microclimate. Another tip for adding humidity is to sit the plants on a pebble-filled saucer of water, which adds moisture and will gently humidify the air while keeping the roots away from stagnant water, which can lead to rot. One of the most common mistakes made with Begonias is overwatering. Only water once the first few centimetres (inches) of soil have dried out if you haven't gone the route of sitting your plant in a pebble-filled tray, and be sure to remove any excess water from its saucer 30 minutes after watering.

Although not all plants kept indoors will flower, the trusty *Begonia* will. And what pretty flowers it has. But with such special foliage, it's by no means just the blooms you're after and many people remove the flowers as they appear to allow the plant to focus its energy on producing new leaves.

Collecting Begonias can quickly become an obsession, and soon enough you'll probably find yourself swapping cuttings with fellow plant fanatics and desperately seeking more and more unusual species. Nanna will be very happy to see them back in action in plant-lovers' homes across the world!

style note

• Go nuts for graphic foliage and pair Begonias with other equally gregarious species, such as *Calathea* (see page 68) and *Maranta*. Let the stripes and spots reign supreme as Anno Leon has done on his covered balcony (see page 212).

the new wave

Now that you've mastered the classics, it's time to move on to the more unusual, harder-to-find plants. A little extra hunting and care is required, but my, oh my, are they worth it.

THE PLANTS

Mini monstera
Rhaphidophora tetrasperma

One look at those petite, graphic leaves and you can see exactly why this guy is referred to as the 'mini monstera'. Other common names include the Philodendron 'ginny' or 'piccolo', but as it so happens the *Rhaphidophora tetrasperma* is neither a Monstera nor a *Philodendron*. This little cutie is actually part of the same Araceae family as Monsteras and Philodendrons, but from a separate genus of plants within the Aroid classification.

Common names aside, however, this stunner is a houseplant seriously in demand! Its lush green leaves, split on opposing sides, make for a dramatic feature plant that looks great sitting alone in a spot that gets lots of bright, indirect light. Fertilising monthly in the warmer seasons will encourage lots of healthy growth, but other than that they're pretty low maintenance.

style note

• Compact in nature, it's a perfect fit for smaller spaces. The Mini monstera is a fast grower and looks great draping from a plant stand or supported with a stake to encourage upward growth. We love them in bedrooms where you can wake up and admire them every morning.

LIGHT
Bright, indirect

WATER
Moderate

SOIL
Well-draining

Peacock plant
Calathea orbifolia

LIGHT
Bright, indirect

WATER
Moderate–high +
misting

SOIL
Well-draining

One of our absolute favourites, the Peacock plant has large, striking, bright-green foliage with silver stripes that grow bigger and bigger with each new leaf. A show-off just like its namesake bird, embrace its fabulously bold foliage and pair with Begonias and Zebra plants for maximum effect in your plant gang.

Of course, all that beauty doesn't come without a little hard work and this prima donna can certainly keep you on your toes. Keep away from cold draughts and air-conditioning, as dry air can cause the tips of the leaves to go brown. Regular misting is appreciated and it's also important to keep the soil consistently moist but not soggy. *Calathea orbifolia* can be quite sensitive to minerals so, if possible, water and mist with purified water or tap water that has been left to sit for 24 hours before use. On this note, wiping the leaves clean with a damp cloth is preferable to using shine sprays – it's nothing but organic for this diva! Yes, it can be high maintenance, but you'll be thanked with glorious beauty day in and day out.

Calathea orbifolia can be propagated every couple of years in spring through a process known as division. Split the root system into two plants and then immediately re-pot into fresh soil. Keep new divisions warm and moist and watch them grow! Soon enough you'll have a whole family of Peacock plants, one for every room.

style note

- *Calathea orbifolia* works well sat alongside other Calatheas. Not only do their mixed leaf patterns create maximum visual effect, placing them together gives you a chance to regularly check on all the high-maintenance plants in one hit.

LIGHT
Bright, indirect

WATER
Moderate

SOIL
Well-draining

Satin pothos
Scindapsus pictus 'Argyraeus'

Although similar in many ways to the good old Devil's ivy with its glorious trailing foliage, the Satin pothos isn't actually a Pothos at all (ah, semantics!). Regardless, its dark-green heart-shaped leaves flecked with a silver smattering of variegation make for a stunning creeper to add to your plant gang.

Like all variegated plants, the mutation will be stronger the more light the plant receives, however it will also survive in lower-light conditions. It's not super fussy, but doesn't like soggy soil or cold draughts. Pruning any sparse vine tips will keep your plant looking bushy and lush, and cuttings can be easily propagated in spring or early summer. It's delightfully pest resistant if looked after properly, but can suffer from root rot if kept too wet, which weakens the plant and opens it up to pests and disease. Avoid overwatering and it should stay pest free.

style note

• In the wild, the Satin pothos climbs up tree trunks or moseys along the ground, but indoors they look great in a hanging pot or jauntily dangling down shelves in your lounge or bedroom.

Horsehead philodendron
Philodendron bipennifolium

LIGHT
Bright, indirect

WATER
Moderate

SOIL
Well-draining

Some of our absolute fave indoor plants are Philodendrons (we're looking at you Heart-leaf and Rojo congo!). Easy to care for and emitting some lovely tropical vibes, what's not to love? If you're after a *Philodendron* a little out of left field, then look no further than the Horsehead or Fiddle leaf philodendron. Sporting elegant, violin-shaped, glossy green leaves that can grow up to 25 cm (10 in) wide and 45 cm (18 in) long, this plant will certainly make a statement in your indoor jungle.

Originating in South America, the Horsehead philodendron is a vining plant that looks fabulous grown on a totem to support its fabulous foliage. No special care notes are necessary for this plant; just the usual bright, indirect light and a solid watering schedule that allows the top layer of soil to dry out between drinks.

style note

- Along with growing up a totem pole, this plant works equally well if allowed to spread out and trail; just make sure you've got the space for this beauty to really make its mark – a spot front and centre in the living room or even on a covered balcony will suit.

style note

• Let this *Philodendron* shine as a stunning statement piece in your living room or bedroom – it adds a wonderfully tropical accent to any well-lit space.

LIGHT
Bright, indirect

WATER
High

SOIL
Moisture-
retaining

Gloriosum
philodendron
Philodendron gloriosum

A velvety goddess, the *Philodendron gloriosum* is a glorious plant indeed. Its large, dramatic leaves unfurl painfully slowly, which only adds to the theatre and suspense. A spreader rather than a climber, it is described as a terrestrial *Philodendron* with leaves emerging from a woody stem that sits at or slightly below the soil surface. The velutinous surface of the heart-shaped leaves are etched with striking pink or silvery white veins that get brighter with age.

The Gloriosum is a slow-growing *Philodendron* that requires a little more maintenance than your standard houseplant, but it's absolutely worth the extra work. Bright light is essential, as is consistently moist soil and high humidity.

Velvet leaf Philodendron
Philodendron micans

A mix of colours and textures can have an incredible impact on an indoor jungle. If you're looking to pair your gorgeous greenery with more unusual-coloured foliage, the Velvet leaf philodendron with its elegant bronze, heart-shaped leaves may be just what you're looking for.

This beauty really stands out, not just for its unusual colouring but also for its velvety texture and the iridescent nature of its leaves. Despite its uniqueness, the aptly named Velvet leaf philodendron is still super easy to care for.

The soil is best kept moist in the warmer months, when it's also great to mist the leaves, but be sure to let it dry out for longer in the cooler months. Although it will thrive in bright, indirect light, it can also cope with lower-light situations.

style notes

• A vine by nature, this *Philodendron* can be trained up a stake or allowed to hang free.

• It can also be easily propagated using stem cuttings, and who wouldn't want more of this moody stunner in their life? Once your cuttings have rooted, plant them in small terracotta pots that allow the velvety leaves to shine.

LIGHT
Bright, indirect

WATER
Moderate +
misting

SOIL
Well-draining

Purple shamrock
Oxalis triangularis

It's crazy to think that this gorgeous and highly in-demand houseplant could inspire anything but pure joy, but the *Oxalis* family is large and a few invasive varieties have given them a bad rap among gardeners. As in most instances, it's important not to judge all varieties by the bad behaviour of a few relatives! It would certainly be a mistake to avoid the *Oxalis triangularis* with its purple butterfly wing-like leaves, which fly from delicate stems and even more poetically open and close in rhythm with the day and night.

style note

• Given the Purple shamrock's bold leaf colour and form, a beautiful neutral-coloured pot will allow the foliage to really pop. We love a textured handmade ceramic; just keep the shape simple.

LIGHT
Bright, indirect

WATER
Moderate when
young, low once
established or
dormant

SOIL
Well-draining

Also known as the Love plant, the Purple shamrock has a similar vibe to Clover, thus explaining its other common name, False shamrock. Along with beautifully delicate foliage, it delivers petite, light purple or white bell-shaped flowers that sit casually above the foliage line. It's one seriously pretty plant and we love seeing it a bit leggy (as opposed to bushy). Embrace a less-symmetrical growth pattern, that way there's no need to rotate it for even growth, as you might with other plants. In full effect, it can reach heights and widths of 50 cm (20 in) and it will have anyone who comes across it seriously swooning.

An oddity of this plant is that it enters a state of dormancy every two to seven years or when it has been neglected or treated poorly. The leaves will die off and the plant will appear dead, but do not fear, as it can spring back to life in just a few short weeks. Cut off all the dead leaves and give the plant a chance to rest, keeping it out of brighter light and watering less until you see a fresh leaf form, at which point you can return it to its usual spot and watering schedule.

Swedish ivy
Plectranthus australis

LIGHT
Bright, indirect

WATER
Moderate

SOIL
Well-draining

Although Swedish ivy plants originally become popular as a houseplant in Sweden and they do have long cascading stems like a regular Ivy plant, this super easy-to-care-for beauty is neither Swedish nor an Ivy! Perfect for novice gardeners, when we say it's easy to look after we really do mean it. This stunning indoor plant will thrive with very little maintenance, providing some seriously good foliage in the process.

  In ideal conditions (bright, indirect light), Swedish ivy will grow rapidly. Just be sure to keep it looking its best with a semi-regular grooming session – trim off yellowing or dead leaves – and shape as desired. Voila!

style note

• A hanging basket will allow the Swedish ivy's luscious foliage to cascade beautifully from a high position and give it the growing space it needs. It will work equally well trailing lushly from a high shelf.

style note

• Do not under any circumstances allow this plant to take a back seat. It's such a rare and unusual beauty that you want to make sure it sits front and centre in a plant cluster, or in a prime position in a more minimally styled room.

LIGHT
Bright, direct

WATER
High

SOIL
Well-draining

Ornamental yam
Dioscorea dodecaneura

Definitely one of the rarest plants you'll see in this book, the Ornamental yam is as beautiful as it is hard to find. This dramatic vine hails from Ecuador and Brazil and sports some sexy variegations on its heart-shaped foliage. The deep-green leaves, which increase in size as the plant matures, are veined with silver and randomly mottled with maroon and black, with the undersides a rich pinkish purple, making it look like a living watercolour painting.

Quirkily, the *Dioscorea dodecaneura* twines in a counterclockwise direction, allowing it to gently grow upwards despite its incredibly dainty stems. In addition to its gorgeous foliage, it produces small, white and perfumed flowers, which bloom in drooping clusters. Sadly you are less likely to witness such blooms indoors, but with leaves this good, who needs flowers!

This plant thrives on plenty of light. It will do well with some direct morning or late afternoon sunlight, with preferably four or more hours of it through an unshaded window. Lots of bright, indirect light will also be tolerated. The Ornamental yam is a thirsty tropical plant, so it needs regular watering. In winter, when temperatures drop, it can go dormant, dying back to its tuberous base. When this happens, stop watering to allow the tubers to almost completely dry out, and start watering again in spring when it will begin its growth cycle again. Resilient to most pests and disease and generally easy to care for, the hardest part will be getting your hands on one!

Swiss cheese vine
Monstera adansonii

LIGHT
Moderate, bright, indirect

WATER
Moderate + misting

SOIL
Well-draining

Another fabulous option for the Monstera obsessed, the Swiss cheese vine is a more delicate (you guessed it) vining cousin of the *Monstera deliciosa* (see page 36). Daintier but no less graphic, it boasts gorgeous, holey leaves that can climb their way up to 20 metres (65 ft) if given the chance. It is often confused with the *Monstera obliqua*, which has slimmer leaves and bigger holes, and is far more rare and elusive than the Adansonii.

The Swiss cheese vine is native to Central and South America and makes a low-maintenance exotic show-stopper for your space. Bright, indirect light conditions should keep it happy and it can be pruned to keep it tidy and full. If you notice the plant getting leggy and the foliage reducing in size, trim it back to encourage fresh growth. Any cuttings that include a leaf node and at least 10 cm/4 in of stem will propagate well in water, or pop it straight into fresh potting mix.

LIGHT

Bright, indirect

WATER

Moderate

SOIL

Well-draining

Variegated Swiss cheese plant
Monstera deliciosa 'variegata'

The appetite for variegated plants seems to be at an all-time high, and one of the most sought-after and difficult to obtain has to be the variegated Monstera. An absolute darling of social media, such is the demand for this plant that cuttings are going for an exorbitant amount of money online. There are two types of cultivated variegated Monsteras: the 'Albo-variegata' which has large splotches of white, and the more dotted 'Thai constellation'. Both are stunning and you would be a lucky plant owner to nab one, let alone both!

The white parts of the leaves are unable to absorb chlorophyll meaning the plant has to work twice as hard to photosynthesise. Generally, this means they will be slower-growing and require more light than their non-variegated counterpart. For this reason, it's important to regularly wipe the leaves (with a wet cloth or in the shower), so it can absorb as much light as possible and maintain its fabulous foliage. Be careful not to over-fertilise, as it is quite sensitive to salt build-up in the soil.

style note

• We love pairing the variegated Monstera with its non-variegated friends to really accentuate the unusual markings of the leaves. You'll be beating jealous plant lovers away with a stick as they hassle you for a precious cutting!

Curly spider plant
Chlorophytum Comosum 'Bonnie'

A houseplant on high rotation in the 70s – think macrame hangers and rattan – the Spider plant definitely went out of favour for a while. Thankfully, as with most things, its popularity has come back around so we can again enjoy this easy-to-care-for plant pal. For something slightly more exotic, 'Bonnie' is the curly cousin of the stalwart Spider plant and it brings some added cuteness to the table. It has all the ease of the common variety, but with added pizzazz. It also happens to be one of NASA's top clean-air plants, so win, win, win.

A member of the Lily family, there are almost 200 varieties of *Chlorophytum*. The most popular variety in the 90s was 'Vittatum', with its broad, white stripe down the centre of each leaf. 'Bonnie' also has these same markings, plus delightful bendy, curly foliage growth. Because Spider plants are so unfussy, they can manage without much light and are often used in bathrooms. Unfortunately for them it means that they are sometimes referred to, not very glamorously, as the toilet plant. But really this curly plant deserves so much more. What makes it so unique is the way it makes its own 'babies', called offsets, which hang below the plant, looking like little spiders. You can simply pluck these off and replant them for easy propagation.

This is a plant that needs very little fertiliser and too much will stop it producing offsets. Keep it evenly moist, but don't overwater or you'll end up with brown leaves. Too much fluoride can also cause the tips to burn, so use purified water when you can. If this does happen, trim the brown ends at an angle with sharp scissors so they still look natural. It's not that fond of the cold, preferring a constant warm temperature.

style note

• Embrace those 70's vibes and let those curly spider babies hang freely from a plant stand.

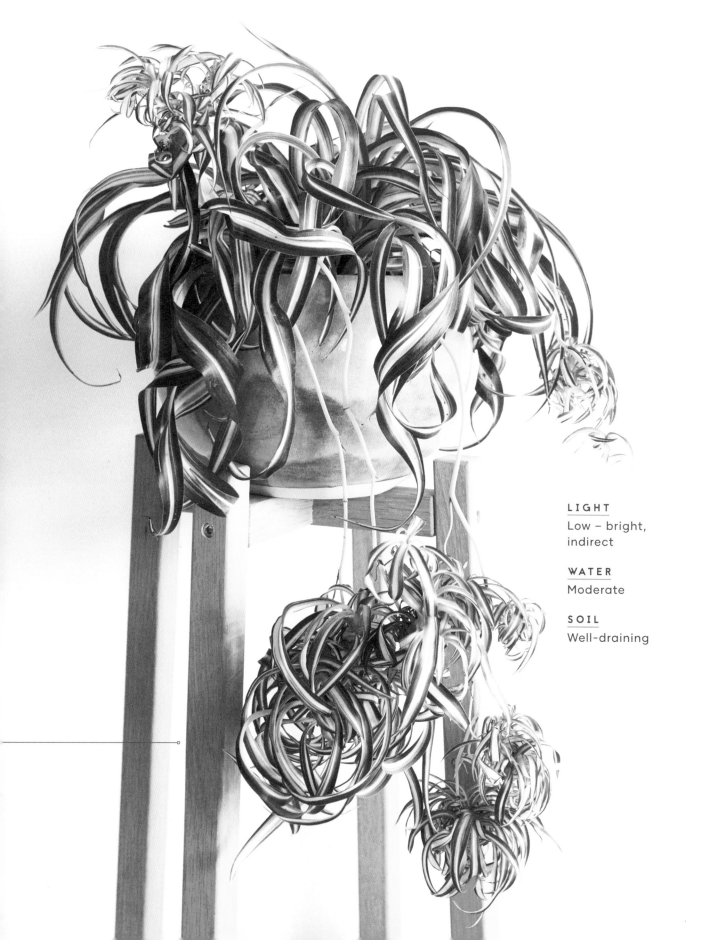

LIGHT
Low – bright,
indirect

WATER
Moderate

SOIL
Well-draining

Zebra alocasia
Alocasia 'Zebrina'

LIGHT
Bright, indirect

WATER
High + misting
in summer

SOIL
Well-draining

Named for its yellow- and black-striped stem, resembling you guessed it, a zebra, the *Alocasia* 'Zebrina' originates from just one Philippine island. This distinctive plant has large, glossy green, arrow-shaped leaves, which will always reach towards the brightest light, so turn the pot occasionally to achieve nice, even growth. Alternatively, allow it to reach towards the light for a more dramatic-shaped plant.

Like other *Alocasia*, the plant will grow quite quickly in the right conditions. Each new stem will grow taller than the last and can reach up to 1 metre (3 feet) in height, making for an incredibly dramatic mature specimen.

Alocasia are notoriously fussy and can frustrate beginner and experienced gardeners alike. The Zebra is demanding when it comes to light and moisture, particularly in summer. Keep it regularly watered during warmer months, but ease off in winter when it's likely to become dormant and die back. It hates having cold feet, so always use lukewarm water when watering. Light misting will generate the humidity it likes, but if water starts dripping from the leaf ends, cut back on watering and increase the light.

style note

- This beauty has stems that are as stunning as its leaves, so be sure to place it in a position that allows all parts of your plant to be admired equally.

PLANT STYLE

Our homes and workspaces can provide a unique opportunity for us to express our personality and style. Just like the colour schemes, artwork, furniture and homewares we choose reflect our aesthetic, so too can the introduction of plants. Unlike the inanimate objects we use for decoration, it is important to differentiate our plants as living things that demand a level of attention our cushions and rugs simply don't. Cultivating an indoor jungle is as much about thoughtfulness and care as it is about style.

YOUR PLANT STYLE

Now that you've assessed your space in more detail, started building a mood board and armed yourself with some of the plant care and maintenance essentials, you're in a great position to start exploring not only the plants that will survive in your space but those that will create the aesthetic of the jungle you want to establish.

When it comes to style, it is always important to follow your instincts. There really are no hard and fast rules so don't feel constrained; it's an opportunity to let your creativity run free. Of course with interiors, things come in and out of fashion, but trust us, your Monstera will continue to bring you happiness long after the copper floor lamp in the corner of the room has gone out of vogue. Steering clear of trends for trends' sake will allow you to focus on introducing elements that truly bring you joy.

It is likely that your space is already a reflection of your style, and so the introduction of plants should complement and elevate the existing elements. See the plants as a beautiful finishing touch, adding a layer of colour and texture to your interiors. Equally, the accessories you bring in to house and style the plants should tie in to your overall vision. From the vessels you choose to pot your plants in to the tools you require to maintain them, they can all be an opportunity to beautify. A brass plant mister can look as cute as a button sitting beside the plant pal that requires spritzing and even the right pair of secateurs can look as good on display as they are useful to have to hand for pruning and propagating.

Some things to consider when styling with plants:

<u>Plant shape, size and growth patterns</u> When it comes to plant placement, consider the shape of a plant (ie. tree-like, upright, vining or trailing) as well as its current size and how it is likely to change as it grows. This can often help determine where it will best work in your space. Plants, such as Rubber plants and Monsteras, are prolific growers needing plenty of room to stretch out. Larger specimens work best as floor plants in simple graphic-patterned pots where their dramatic and impressive foliage can be fully appreciated. Trailing plants such as Pothos or Chain of hearts sit beautifully on plant stands, atop shelves or suspended in hanging pots cascading towards the floor.

<u>Plant pairings</u> Grouping plants with similar care needs can save time and also create microclimates that benefit them. It's good to think about combining different foliage textures, growth patterns and vessels for interest. When space is at a premium, small clusters of plants dotted around a room on tables and shelves can be very effective, increasing the greenery factor even in smaller apartments. Groups of three and five plants tend to be more visually appealing than those of even numbers.

<u>Textures and patterning of foliage</u> Combining a mix of patterned, textured or colourful foliage (think Begonias, Calathea and ferns) with plants featuring simpler, more graphic leaves adds depth and interest to your indoor jungle. If you want to be really bold, a combination of highly patterned plants is the way to go.

choosing the right vessel

FROM HANDMADE CERAMIC PLANTERS to aged terracotta urns, when it comes to pairing plants with their ideal vessels, the whole really is more than the sum of its parts. Choosing the perfect homes for your plants is both a visual and functional consideration. From a practical point of view, the planter must facilitate good plant maintenance – that is, preferably providing adequate drainage and a means of easily watering your plant as well as providing enough room for the root system with a little growing space. Visually, the pot or planter you choose can elevate your foliage as well as creating a cohesive look for your indoor jungle.

Particularly when shopping at your local nursery, it is likely that many of your plants will arrive at your home in a plastic pot. Although not visually inspiring, these basic containers provide excellent drainage for plants and there is really no need to repot them immediately, unless you can already see roots escaping out of the base or you have a specific pot in mind that it can be directly planted into. One of the easiest ways to cover the plastic pot is to sit it inside a cache pot. This outer pot will generally not have drainage holes but should be big to comfortably hide the plastic pot within it. You can then water your plants in situ (saving a lot of trips to the kitchen sink); just don't forget to empty out any excess water that may be sitting in the cache pot 30 minutes after watering.

When choosing pots, it makes sense to think about your interior style, homewares and the existing colour palette of your space. The style of the vessels you choose for your indoor plants should complement the aesthetic of your home as well as enhance the plants which they will house. If your style is bold and eclectic, it stands to reason that you may introduce pots with bright colours and patterns. Just keep in mind that the pot should show the foliage in its best light – anything variegated or heavily textured may be overwhelmed in a very busy pot. In these instances, a more neutral or organic look will allow the plant to really shine.

It's a good idea to think about how your plants and pots will sit together within your space. Sticking to one style of pot (such as terracotta) in a range of differing sizes can be incredibly effective. If you're anything like us, with an addiction to collecting beautiful handmade ceramic planters, think about how you will group planters with complementary shapes, textures and finishes. Variations in form of both the vessels and plants can provide interest, especially when creating clusters of plants within your space. We love shopping both locally and further afield with small businesses and makers. It is a wonderful way to source unique pots and it feels fantastic to support creatives who put an incredible amount of soul into crafting beautiful handmade objects.

‹ Indoor foliage comes in myriad shapes and textures. We love the star-shaped growth on this *Anthurium polyschistum*, commonly known as the Faux marijuana plant.

some other vessels to consider ...

• **Self-watering pots** In these pots, water is drawn up into the soil of the plant from a reservoir in the base of the pot. They work particularly well for those very thirsty plants in your gang, think Boston and Maidenhair ferns, that enjoy consistently moist soil. They are also handy for those who are often travelling for work and are perhaps not able to water as regularly as needed.

• **Hanging pots** These vessels are fabulous for showcasing lush, trailing foliage, allowing it to cascade down towards the ground. Be sure the pots are well supported with a hook drilled into a strong beam or hanging from a solid rail.

> Rattan and woven baskets, such as these beauties on display in Byron Bay's Nikau Store, make a great lightweight cache pot to house your plants. Just make sure you place a saucer in the bottom to catch any excess water runoff.

The placement of plants within your space can often help dictate the types of vessels you need to source. You may be looking to fill a large empty corner with a very mature indoor tree. In this case you want to consider the weight of the potted plant as well as how you will be watering it. It can be a good idea to opt for a lightweight concrete-look pot rather than something more solid. Consider sitting the plant in its plastic pot with a saucer within the outer pot to not only facilitate watering but so that it can be easily moved to another spot if necessary. If you decide on direct planting, be aware that the plant will be much more difficult to shift and will require a saucer underneath to catch excess when watering.

Larger feature plants look fantastic in simple geometric pots that create a strong visual base but allow the plant to take centre stage. Often available in white, black and concrete, or painted with simple graphic patterns, they can create a beautiful statement without fighting with the other elements of your interior. When grouping a few plants of varying sizes, sticking to neutral pot colours but in a few different shapes can be quite effective. Egg-shaped planters, tall cylinders and short round bowls can work beautifully when tied together by a cohesive colour scheme and selection of plants. Grouping plants of similar care requirements not only works visually but also helps when it comes to plant maintenance. A large tropical *Strelitzia* would pair perfectly with a Monstera and a large *Philodendron*. All will thrive in bright, indirect light and the mix of foliage shapes and plant-growth patterns are a wonderful match.

In addition to more traditional pots, we love incorporating texture with woven baskets that are incredibly practical for covering plastic plant pots. These relatively inexpensive and lightweight pot covers are especially useful in more transient jungles (hello, renters), or for those with a propensity for constantly shifting their plants around to suit their mood. Rattan is another organic material that works particularly well for housing indoor plants. Huge back in the 70s when house plants were *de rigueur*, this decidedly retro look is absolutely back in fashion, and there are some incredible rattan plant stands available that look fantastic filled with greenery.

tool kit

WHAT IS IT THEY SAY? That someone is only as good as their tools? With the right equipment, caring for and styling your indoor jungle can be a whole lot more enjoyable and effective. Here are some of our go-to implements.

Secateurs or scissors Handy for pruning dead foliage as well as making clean cuts when propagating. They are also good for jobs like trimming stakes down to size. Be sure to keep them super sharp and clean.

Watering can You may need a few different sizes but at least one with a long fine spout for accurate delivery of water to the soil is ideal. Fill with water again after emptying to ensure you always have pure water on hand.

Water mister Providing your tropical humidity-loving plants with some moisture on their foliage is easily done with a mister or spray bottle. Morning is the best time for spritzing, but be sure to provide good ventilation so that water isn't left to sit stagnant on the foliage.

Moisture meter There are many of these on the market and they're a foolproof way of knowing when your plants need watering. Some are designed to stay in the soil while others can be used as you water. If you're high-tech, opt for one that connects to an app on your phone. Fancy!

Apron, gloves + mask When dealing with soil (during potting in particular) some good protective clothing is essential. An apron will keep clothes clean, and gloves and a mask will prevent you from ingesting or inhaling any nasties found in potting mix.

Potting tray Especially for those of us in apartments who may be potting our plants inside, a shallow box or tray can help keep the mess at bay.

Dustpan For anything that spills out of the potting tray, a dustpan will quickly get rid of the rest. Sweep up soil and dead leaves with ease.

Plant stands Add height variation to your indoor jungle and get plants up off the floor or table with stands. Available in a variety of materials but most commonly seen in timber and metal.

Hooks Whether you're training a vine up and across a wall or supporting hanging planters, hooks of varying shapes and sizes are a useful addition to your plant styling kit.

Pots + vessels The possibilities are literally endless here (and we explore the options in more detail on page 97), but pairing a plant with its perfect home is both a functional and aesthetic consideration that can allow a plant to truly flourish.

Plant stakes Essential for supporting upright growth and training vining plants, these can come in a variety of materials and thicknesses. From skinny bamboo sticks to chunky moss poles, simply anchor in the soil, attach to a strong central stem with twine or thin wire and your plant will grow up, up and away.

PLANT STYLE: ROOM BY ROOM

When it comes to creating your indoor jungle, as far as we're concerned there's not a room in the house that can't benefit from the inclusion of some greenery. Bringing plants into each of your spaces will always be dictated by the light and temperature conditions available, but within those parameters there are myriad ways that plants breathe life into an interior. In the following pages we go room by room to show you how to thoughtfully incorporate plants into every nook and cranny. Greenery can be the most amazing finishing touch to your interiors, adding shape, colour, texture and harmony to complement your aesthetic and provide that important connection to nature.

In the bedroom

BEDROOMS ARE THE SPACES in our homes in which it is most important for us to create a relaxed sanctuary, and are thus perfect for the introduction of some lush greenery. With their ability to really soften a space and foster a sense of calm, plants work beautifully in the places we sleep. Plants that are particularly good at detoxifying the air, such as Devil's ivy, Spider plants and Snake plants, are great options to ensure you're breathing easy and getting the best sleep you can.

For a large bedroom, opt for sculptural feature plants in big beautiful pots mixed in with some plants on stands for height variation. To play with scale you can position smaller plants on bedside tables or tumbling down the sides of dressers. Try hanging beauties from hooks in the ceiling, or make use of what's available and hang along curtain railings.

Even if your bedroom is small you don't have to sacrifice the lushness. A high shelf above the bed with trailing tropicals is a beautiful option and an amazing feature. Opposite, horticulturist Thomas Denning has created this stylish plant shelf above the master bed (see more of his plant-filled Melbourne apartment on page 204). Here are some tips for making one work in your space.

1 Make sure all pots have saucers (the deeper the better) to allow any excess from watering to be caught, avoiding wet bedding at all costs.

2 Ensure the shelves are professionally installed and can take the weight of the potted plants; waking up to a plant falling on your head is the opposite of relaxing!

3 Create texture and depth to the collection with an interesting selection of greenery rather than just sticking to one type.

4 Opt for plants that have slightly lower water needs as it can be a little tricky to get up there to water every couple of days. And let's face it, dead plants are not going to create the jungle vibes of your dreams. Species of Pothos, *Rhipsalis*, *Hoya*, and Chain of hearts are all great to have in the mix, with the added bonus that they trail beautifully.

To complement larger plants
and add a sense of scale,
smaller specimens look fabulous
on a bedside table, as seen in
the home of Nick Simonyi (see
more on page 222).

style notes

• A mix of trailing and upright plants create shape and interest on this bedside table.

• Small plants stands are ideal for this compact spot. An airplant in a small ceramic vessel sits daintily under the bedside lamp.

style note

• In a spacious living area, mature plants of varying foliage shapes can create a wonderfully textured jungle vibe. Mix in full trailing plants, as seen here at London photographic studio Clapton Tram, to create a layered effect with greenery reaching from floor to ceiling.

In the living room

A SPACE TO GATHER, socialise, eat, relax or just be, this is generally the room where we spend most of our time, so what better place to really let loose and fulfil your greatest jungle desires! For those with the time and inclination to maintain some serious lushness, the living room, which is often one of the larger spaces in the house, is the place to do it. Those with less room can introduce a sculptural statement plant such as a mature Bird *Strelitzia* or a dramatic *Dracaena* in an empty corner without sacrificing too much precious floor space. An indoor tree like a large Sabre fig is another beautiful option for a bright corner spot or to create an impressive centrepiece for a room. Where more established plants will overwhelm a room (or in addition to larger foliage) you can mix in a variety of smaller plants clustered on coffee tables and shelves. Softening large furniture units with greenery can help to camouflage some of the less beautiful elements in this room, such as the TV.

When it comes to choosing your hero or feature plants, healthy, lush specimens will look the most impressive. Go big or go home, as they say! Graphic foliage like that of a Monstera or the Horsehead philodendron stand out beautifully against a simple background. The contrast of green leaves on a white wall is really strong – or why not up the jungle factor with a bold shade of green paint on the wall? Try and keep a feature plant in a clutter-free spot with a bit of breathing space so it can truly shine. You'll definitely want to keep these large plants looking their best by regularly wiping down their leaves, which will gather dust just like your furniture. Another great living room hero is the Pothos, trained to cover a wall. Fast-growing vining plants in the right conditions will spread out quickly and are best attached to the wall with small clear removable hooks that will disappear beneath the foliage and create an incredible living surface.

To create a plant cluster, always place the largest plants at the back and then layer medium and smaller plants as you work your way towards the front. You can add in plant stands to help create these different heights. Play with plants that have different leaf sizes and textures, adding pops of lighter green among darker leaves, and make sure to include plants with interesting leaf patterns and variegations. You want to use more upright plants – vines won't work well sitting on the ground and anything too wide will appear too bulky in the mix. Always be sure that leaves aren't touching and that your plants are close but still have room to breathe. Because of their proximity, clustering has the added benefit of creating a microclimate around these plants, boosting humidity and creating ease of watering!

style note

- Some of our favourite stand-alone living room plants include Rubber plants, Monsteras and Palms. All are used to incredible effect in this light-filled Berlin apartment (see more on page 132).

In the kitchen

WHILE THE KITCHEN may not be the first place you think of to incorporate indoor greenery, there are many instances where plants can feature to incredible effect. If you're lucky enough to have a bright sunny spot in the kitchen, a container herb garden is a great idea for keeping your ingredients close at hand. We keep tarragon (great with roast chicken), parsley (to sprinkle on almost anything), basil (grows best in the warmer months and goes great on pizza), thyme (for soups) and mint (to freshen up salads and cold drinks). Other yummy herbs include dill, oregano, lemongrass, chives, coriander (cilantro) and the slightly more unusual perilla (shiso), marjoram and chervil. We can't imagine buying herbs from the supermarket ever again.

You don't have to stop at edible plants in the kitchen as your tropical greens work just as well. Think styles that won't take up precious benchtop space – a tall but slim floor-sitting tree or petite pots lining your windowsill. Plants hung from the ceiling are also a great space saver. Aloe vera is a wonderful plant for the kitchen as the gel it produces soothes and cools burns that might result from a little kitchen mishap. It's also fun to think outside the box – how about popping an avocado seed or a whole sweet potato (just make sure they haven't been sprayed) into propagating vases and watch them sprout. Nature can be so damn amazing, and checking in to see how they've grown every morning as you make your cup of tea is a pretty special thing to do.

A few things to be aware of:

1   Keep plants clear of heat from ovens and cooktops, as they aren't fans of big changes in temperature or getting burnt!

2   Keep cleaning chemicals away from anything you're planning on eating.

3   Avoid plants that will grow too large. Space is usually at a premium in kitchens and you don't want to bump into anything while your arms are loaded with that evening's stew.

style notes

• When space is at a premium in a smaller kitchen a hanging plant can introduce greenery without taking up bench space.

• Make the most of a bright windowsill with smaller potted plants. This can be a great spot for edibles so they are close to hand for use in cooking.

In the bathroom

BATHROOMS HAVE TWO THINGS going for them when it comes to plant placement: proximity to a water source and higher levels of humidity created from showers and baths. Moisture- and humidity-loving plants, such as ferns, orchids and Spider plants, will do well in such conditions. One thing to note is the potential for an especially hot steamy shower to cause damage to some delicate or sensitive foliage, so opt for hardier specimens, such as the Macho fern, which will be better equipped to deal with any dramatic shifts in temperature. Adequate ventilation will be very much appreciated by your bathroom-dwelling plants, too, and can prevent soil from staying too moist or foliage remaining damp and potentially open to the development of fungus and mould issues.

Due to the need for privacy, bathrooms tend to be lower-light spaces and so it is important to consider introducing plants that are more tolerant of these conditions, such as Hoyas or Pothos. If you're one of the lucky ones blessed with a beautifully lit bathroom, perhaps from a skylight or high window, using this space for propagating can be an interesting way to create a pretty feature without taking up too much space. You'll need a collection of small clean glass bud-style vases that will fit neatly on a windowsill or small shelf. Take clean cuttings from your existing plants and place them into water, ensuring no leaves are sitting below the water line. Your cuttings should root in a few weeks, at which point you can continue to let them grow or re-pot them, creating a new plant to add to the gang. Just be sure to keep these sensitive cuttings away from intense light.

In small bathrooms, such as en suites, try introducing more petite greenery and making use of existing elements for plant placement. Utilising shower curtain rails or hooks suctioned to tiles for hanging or wall-mounted plants is a beautiful way to style your bathroom when space is at a premium. Elkhorn or Staghorn ferns, native orchids and other epiphytes (plants that grow on other plants or surfaces and derive their nutrients from debris, air and water instead of soil) are all fabulous choices. For renters trying to disguise an older-style bathroom interior – or just some less-attractive bathroom features – plants can hide a multitude of sins. A trailing plant on top of the cistern or a small cluster of plants on an ugly vanity can provide a lush distraction.

In the workspace

WE SPEND A LARGE PORTION of our lives at work and if that space is uninspiring and devoid of beauty, it can be pretty damn unmotivating. Thankfully, many employers are recognising the benefits a beautiful workspace can have on creativity, productivity and staff morale, and plants most definitely have an important role to play. A UK study (published in the *Journal of Experimental Psychology: Applied* in 2014) found that productivity increased by 15 per cent in workplaces where plants were introduced. Other studies have proved the link between plants and an increased sense of well-being and boosted self-esteem.

Visually, plants not only bring life and colour to the workplace, but offer an almost meditative experience that, ultimately, leads to happier and healthier employees. The realm of biophilic design explores the importance of humans maintaining a connection to the natural world within the built environment. Green office spaces have been seen to generate physiological responses, such as increased brain activity and lower stress hormones.

Sadly, not all of us are lucky enough to spend our days tinkering away in light-filled converted warehouse spaces filled with greenery. Many offices are often lacking in natural light and fresh air (two things plants really love) and the plants that do make their way inside can end up looking very sad indeed. Thankfully there are some options that will survive in these less-than-desirable conditions and can, in turn, make your working environment a more pleasant one. Kentia palms, Zanzibar gems, Snake plants, Peace lilies and Pothos are all mainstays of the office environment, as they will tolerate lower-light conditions and even survive a little neglect. If you have a more plant-friendly, well-lit and well-ventilated environment, why not try some more unusual varieties, such as Hoyas, ferns, Marble queen pothos or the trusty Monstera, to really impress any visiting clients.

Larger plants scattered throughout a working space provide interest and something soothing for workers to gaze at when taking breaks from staring at their screens all day. Plants can also be used to screen off or differentiate areas, providing lush privacy in meeting and break areas. In warehouse spaces, utilising beams for hanging plants can create a strong feature without taking up room on desks that may be limited. Where there is space for desk plants, smaller specimens of Snake and Spider plants can thrive even under fluorescent lighting. Make it easy for staff to water by selecting pots with drainage and saucers.

care note

- Make sure you implement a watering roster so plants don't get neglected (or overwatered!). Be sure to check in regularly with the plants to ensure factors such as air conditioning aren't allowing plants to dry out too quickly.

A Moroccan-inspired courtyard is central to La Porte Deux's co-working space in Sydney. They have created a veritable oasis in the city with rustic oversized pots filled with Agave, *Strelitzia* and lemon trees. Rattan outdoor furniture complements the look and ties the whole space together.

The outside room

FOR THOSE OF US living in apartments, balconies and courtyards become extensions of our interiors – an outdoor room – if you will. Planting in these spaces not only creates a more beautiful outlook from inside and masking or screening from neighbouring buildings, it also increases the enjoyment of the spaces themselves. It's far more pleasant to relax on a lush balcony softened by greenery than on a sparse tiled space surrounded by concrete. Whether an area is covered or open to the elements, there is an abundance of plants to suit your circumstances.

An open courtyard or balcony is the perfect opportunity to explore some beautiful sun-loving foliage. *Bougainvillea* and *Wisteria*, for example, do brilliantly in full sun and look incredible trained up a trellis or wire. Cacti and Succulents are another great choice in a full-sun position as most will happily soak up precious rays. Beautifully graphic and perfect for creating a Palm Springs-inspired scene, why not try *Agave, Euphorbia, Cereus* or *Crassula* (check out the rooftop at the Paramount Recreation Club on page 120 for inspiration). There are also lots of 'indoor' plants that happily tolerate sunnier conditions, such as *Strelitzia*, and you can always move some of your indoor plants to sunnier climes during winter to ensure that they receive the light they require for healthy photosynthesis when it's darker indoors.

Edible plants will love a sunny position outside, so why not create your own kitchen container garden filled with herbs and smaller veggies. Potted citrus, from a standard lemon or lime to something more exotic, such as a Buddha's hand, look fantastic in large vessels. Dwarf varieties are also great for smaller spaces. Edible flowers, such as Ruffled pansies and Golden marigold, can provide spectacular colour if that tickles your fancy. Scent is also a lovely sense to explore in a balcony or courtyard garden setting. Lavender evokes the south of France and Jasmine takes you straight to the streets of Southeast Asia.

When choosing pots for outside, make sure you pick harder-wearing ones than you would for indoors. Opt for materials that weather nicely when exposed to rain and sun, and ensure that plants have adequate drainage. There is less need for saucers outside, as water can usually run off into drains, but it can be useful to cover drainage holes with some fly screen or mesh when potting up to keep soil from escaping when watering.

Plants, too, are obviously more exposed when living outdoors so beware of wind and scorching sun that can burn or tear leaves. Like your indoor spaces, make sure you do a proper assessment of the environment and choose plants that will thrive in those specific conditions.

Covered balconies that provide plenty of shelter from harsher weather can be a perfect home to many of the plants you may be keeping inside. It may be one of the brightest areas of your home and thus the ideal spot to create your jungle. Vertical gardens are also increasingly popular, while outdoor shelving can be used to equally strong effect to house collections of smaller plants for those unable to attach elements to the walls. Larger feature pots housing palms, Elephant ears and Philodendrons create a strong foundation when mixed in with Begonias, Tradescantias and Hostas, which bring the pattern and colour. Utilise outdoor furniture for plant placement or look at installing hooks to hang some beautiful trailers such as the Macho fern or Chain of hearts.

At the Paramount Recreation Club in Sydney the rooftop has been given a Palm Springs aesthetic with a mix of Succulents and Cacti that suit the exposed conditions.

style note

• Block out traffic noise
and close neighbours in an
inner city apartment with
greenery that extends to
a covered balcony. You can
design your ideal view just
as stylist Jono Felming has
done with mature Elephant
ears, Philodendrons and an
array of potted Succulents.
(See more of his lush urban
jungle on pg 178.)

THE JU

NGLES

From wild, overgrown warehouse conversions to more minimally decorated apartments, we explore how plants interact with the spaces they find themselves in. Peeking into the homes and work places of plant lovers from around the world provides invaluable inspiration for your own indoor jungle. The passion and dedication of these indoor gardeners is catching, and reading about their love for and experience with plants provides useful insights into how to cultivate your own jungle paradise.

GREEN

John Bassam + his dog, Jack

CONVERSION

Once a Victorian horse-drawn tram depot, this stylish warehouse conversion in East London is now a lush photography studio. And when we say lush, we mean seriously packed with greenery. Painted white brickwork, patterned concrete floors and exposed beams are the perfect backdrop for the multitude of plants that fill the beautifully lit space. Known as Clapton Tram, this incredible historic site has been given a new life hosting events and photoshoots alike. Who wouldn't want to get hitched surrounded by all that foliage? John Bassam and his gorgeous border collie, Jack, are the caretakers of the space and responsible for keeping the jungle alive. Choosing to focus on easy-care foliage, such as Monsteras and Spider plants, and avoiding Succulents that don't do well in the space are John's keys to success. And what's the secret to watering all those hanging plants? Lots of ladders!

THE JUNGLES

THE JUNGLES   green conversion

Green on green on green is the go at John's studio, with a fabulous olive couch surrounded on every side by lush Monsteras, Boston ferns, Spider plants and Devil's ivy.

By hanging plants from the exposed beams, John has made great use of the space, drawing the eye up and creating a wonderful curtain of green around the window.

style notes

• While greenery definitely pops off a white wall, why not be bold and opt for green paint in certain zones? Green on green in varying shades can be beautifully effective.

• Create a lush corner spot surrounded by large feature plants. Palms frame this stunning rattan chair perfectly.

THE BOTANICAL

Tim Labenda, fashion designer + partner, Hannes Krause

APARTMENT

BERLIN, GERMANY

Forget minimalism, for German fashion designer Tim and his partner Hannes a home must be comfortable and habitable, but that doesn't mean it can't also be beautiful. Their Berlin apartment, shared with black poodle Putin, is a reflection of their combined personalities and aesthetics. Adorned with a mix of vintage furniture, pieces collected over time and perhaps most importantly, plants, it is truly a product of its inhabitants. Large windows provide the perfect light conditions for their incredible collection of greenery. Mature Monsteras, Philodendrons and Palms thrive, having been chosen for their robustness, opulence and the serious jungle vibes they create. Trips across Germany have been taken by the pair to procure the perfect specimens, meaning each one has its own beautiful backstory. It is this authenticity that shines through in their space and creates a relaxed, yet luxurious, environment.

THE JUNGLES

Tim and Hannes' beautifully
curated collection of vintage
and designer objects sit perfectly
alongside their plants both potted
and propagating in water.

WHERE DOES YOUR LOVE OF PLANTS STEM FROM?

I think it's all the fault of Phoebe Philo. She's the ex-creative director of the fashion label Celine, who incorporated lots of plants into the design of their stores. When I first visited one of her stores, I fell so deeply in love with the idea of having plants around that I started collecting them.

HOW HAVE YOU LEARNED TO KEEP YOUR PLANTS SO BEAUTIFULLY HEALTHY?

I basically learned by living with them. Every one needs a different treatment and some are needier than others. I think in general it's always good if they have a lot of light, and a careful use of water. The best thing is to listen to their needs and treat every one in its own way.

WHY DO YOU THINK IT'S IMPORTANT TO BRING GREENERY INTO A SPACE?

Plants make every space welcoming and pleasant. For me in our environment, I love this idea of creating a tropical, oriental vibe. Our plants look super rich and opulent, which I really adore and I also think they show our other interior pieces in a better light and setting.

DOES YOUR LOVE OF PLANTS INFLUENCE YOUR CREATIVE WORK?

Sometimes. I once did a collection dedicated to Matisse's paper cut-outs, which mainly featured Monstera leaves.

YOU CLEARLY HAVE AN INTEREST IN INTERIOR DESIGN AS WELL AS FASHION. TELL US ABOUT YOUR STYLE/AESTHETIC.

I love the idea of a decadent but affordable interior presented in an easy and welcoming way. I do not like places where you don't know if you're allowed to sit, because everything is so clean and ordered. That's why I styled our apartment in a light, colourful and plant-filled way. I really like the boho, *1001 nights* (Middle Eastern folk tale) aesthetic with a touch of Chateau Marmont in LA! The plants I have chosen are mostly large and luxurious because I think big leaves look more opulent than having a million mini plants. That's why I have so many Palms, Monsteras and Philodendrons, including a big Xanadu as well as a Bird of paradise.

Large, established plants with sizeable leaves add to the grandeur of the high ceilings and big bay windows in the Berlin apartment.

"I love the idea of a decadent but affordable interior ... that's why I styled our apartment in a light, colourful and plant-filled way."

WHAT'S YOUR TOP STYLING TIP FOR BRINGING GREENERY INTO A SPACE?

A dark wall will set all your greenery on fire! I think all those greens look amazing in front of darker colours.

HOW DO YOU GO ABOUT CHOOSING PLANTS TO ADD TO YOUR COLLECTION AND HOW LONG HAS IT TAKEN TO BUILD YOUR JUNGLE?

It has taken me about four years now. I started with a big Monstera, which I bought from an old lady. The plant was already 20 years old, in great condition and has amazing genes. I have so many seedlings from her that our whole apartment is more or less covered with her offspring. I chose the others because of their leaves and size – I really love all their different leaf shapes and shades of green.

WHERE DO YOU FIND INSPIRATION FOR BOTH YOUR DESIGN PRACTICE AND INDOOR JUNGLE?

Basically in nature and on my travels. I really enjoy discovering new places, cities, glasshouses and botanical gardens. I think inspiration can be found everywhere; you just need to keep your eyes open!

Large plants form the basis of Tim and Hannes's jungle but smaller specimens dot the shelving to soften the space and create styled vingettes.

style notes

• A dark wall makes a bold and dramatic background for foliage. Incorporating a mix of different coloured and patterned foliage will add even more depth and interest to the space.

• To pump up the foliage factor without extra plants to keep alive, introduce decorative botanical elements and artwork.

STRANGE PLANT

Jane Rose Lloyd, horticulturalist

GLASSHOUSE

MELBOURNE, AUSTRALIA

A crazy plant lady in every sense of the title, chlorophyll runs through the veins of the incredibly inspiring Jane Rose Lloyd. Horticulturist, producer, researcher and obsessed plant collector and educator, Jane has created the most wonderful foliage-filled sanctuary in her home in the foothills of the Dandenong Ranges, just east of Melbourne. Carefully cultivating indoor plants is clearly her passion, as is helping people understand and appreciate the delicate interactions between individuals, plants and place. She is an absolute fountain of plant knowledge and her home and greenhouse are testament to her obsession. From the outside, Jane's house looks like an average-looking 60s Australian home, but this suburban gem sports spectacular large windows and floods of natural light, making it the perfect growing space for an enviable collection of weird and wonderful indoor plants that typically amount to 150–200 at any given time!

A corner shelf is the perfect stage for Jane's collection of rare and wonderful plants, while proximity to those vast windows ensures a bright environment for her more light-loving plants.

TELL US ABOUT YOURSELF...

I was born in tropical Queensland, and have often wondered if my DNA was somehow botanically altered or influenced at birth. I moved to Melbourne at a very young age, where I was raised in and around the leafy inner-northern suburbs by my incredible mum who taught me almost everything I know about working hard for what you want. And just like my mum, I don't stop. I'm always doing something with plants, whether I've clocked on for work or am taking a day off. i get to work with incredible and fascinating plants every day — growing and caring for them, delivering them to excited customers or shipping them off to new homes interstate, researching and teaching about their funny little quirks and adaptations, but most of all just being with them — and it has got to be one of the most rewarding and nurturing jobs on earth. On the rare chance I decide to take a day off, I typically indulge my non-indoor plant cravings, usually by exploring pine plantations, native sclerophyll forests, botanical gardens and glasshouses or national parks.

YOU'RE A HORTICULTURIST AND AN AVID PLANT LOVER. WHERE DID YOUR LOVE OF PLANTS COME FROM?

Chlorophyll is in my blood; I think I am part plant! As a small child I spent most of my time in my Oma's garden, where I first developed a passion for plants and dirt. Growing up, Mum always made sure we had a garden, and she liked to grow orchids. I remember large pots of Cymbidiums sitting by the front and back doors which would flower most years, and Oncidiums were and still are her favourite cut flowers. My grandpa Charlie loved his garden more than anything and his peach trees were his pride and joy, and my papa had the most wonderful sheoaks (*Casuarina sp.*), which were as tall as houses and dripping with Spanish moss (*Tillandsia usneoides*). When I sit down and think about it, plants have held a prominent place in my family for as long as I can remember. We all connect with plants in some way or another; we all love spending time with our hands in dirt, and we all love the Australian bush. We are a family of the land and we all really treasure and appreciate that. Helping others remember and reclaim this connection is one of the most rewarding aspects of my job.

YOU'VE BEEN QUITE OPEN ABOUT YOUR STRUGGLES WITH MENTAL HEALTH. DO YOU BELIEVE PLANTS CAN HAVE POSITIVE EFFECTS ON HEALTH AND WELLBEING?

I would be so happy to be the poster woman for the positive relationship between plants and mental health. I'm all for talking about it. I've experienced a life-long journey with mental-health issues and I know I will never be completely free of them, but discovering plants truly saved my life. They helped me to understand my purpose and

There's no hiding Jane's obsession with plants. Hanging from curtain rails (who needs curtains anyway!) and sitting on every surface, this is the perfect green view to wake up to each morning.

have given me something I will happily spend the rest of my life doing. Not only is there countless research attesting to the many positive effects plants have on human health and wellbeing, I could easily write a book about all the stories I've gathered over the years from those I've met who have had similar experiences; people who also collect or work with plants and the long list of life improvements they all attribute to nurturing their green thumb. Of all the various methods of therapy and counselling I've tried in over five years, plants have been the most consistently beneficial form of therapy. For me, plants are magical!

Having plants around me makes me feel safe and comfortable. They make my house feel the most like a home. My plants are what I watch while the TV is on, and they are what I listen to when I fall asleep. That feeling when you get to watch new growth right in front of your eyes, knowing that all the thoughtful caring, watering and whispering sweet nothings was not too much but just right is indescribable and incredibly rewarding.

WHAT IS IT ABOUT LIVING AND WORKING WITH PLANTS THAT YOU FIND SO INSPIRING?

Plants inspire me every day in so many ways. I love exploring how far I can push their environmental tolerances. Of all the things I've learned from my countless hours of research, it is a plant's endless drive towards adaptability that I find the most inspiring. The way that plants are forced to constantly adapt to adversity and change while continuing to grow is one of the most valuable plant lessons I've learned. We really are just like them.

YOU'VE GOT AN ENVIABLE COLLECTION OF WEIRD AND WONDERFUL INDOOR PLANTS. HOW MANY DO YOU CURRENTLY OWN? AND HOW MUCH WORK IS INVOLVED IN KEEPING THEM ALL HAPPY AND HEALTHY?

I'm not 100 per cent sure how many plants I own, as they're always coming and going, but it typically hovers around 150–200 of my own. I grow and source plants for the business and have been known to keep the odd one for myself, or I'll grow something special to divide and propagate. I also revive plants for friends, care for some private collections and contract grow for a few special people. However, I still kill plants! And I love that I'm constantly learning from them. Caring for all of these plants is honestly a full-time job, and sometimes it does feel like work (probably because it is). But most of the time it's free therapy. I wine and dine a new plant when I get it home, try to get to know it and understand where it slots into my care regime. I spend a couple of hours a few times a week inspecting, checking, sticking fingers in soil, watering and fertilising my plants. I often talk to them and always make sure to play them classical music at least once a week. Good vibes only – it makes all the difference.

From Hoyas and Dragon tail plants to velutinous Alocasias, Jane tenderly cares for all her plant babies.

style note

• Plants are a great way to disguise less flashy features in your home or workspace. Throw a Boston fern (a great humidity-loving choice for a bathroom) on a cistern and your eye will instantly be drawn to the beautiful greenery rather than anything else.

JAMIE'S

Jamie Song, co-director of online vintage gallery
Bureau of Interior Affairs + La La the cat

JUNGLE

LONDON, UNITED KINGDOM

A converted hydraulic pumping station built in 1902 is home for Jamie Song, his two business partners, La La the cat and over 100 gorgeous houseplants. It's a multi-functional space including an art gallery, workspace and warehouse. The beautiful interior features white bricks, metal beams and high ceilings, but one of its most notable attributes is an enormous skylight. Flooding the spacious warehouse with natural light, it accentuates the period features of the site and provides the perfect conditions for keeping happy houseplants. Jamie has been building his glorious collection of greenery since moving to the space in 2013. So much more than merely decorative elements, Jamie views his plants as 'nature's works of art'. He incorporates them into his home's décor, alongside the human-created works of art for his vintage gallery business.

   Accruing such a jungle has been a huge learning curve; an ongoing experiment to discover the species that thrive (and those that don't), and it has developed into quite an obsession. Finding himself at the starting line of the houseplant phenomenon, he posts about his plant exploits on Instagram where @jamies_jungle has built a loyal following of fellow plant lovers, with over 184,000 at the last count!

THE JUNGLES

White brick provides the
perfect backdrop for Jamie's
collection of art and plants.
Here, Mistletoe cactus,
silvery leaves and flowering
orchids bring life and energy
to the space.

YOU DESCRIBE YOURSELF AS 'A PLANT HOARDER IN THE MODERN BOHEMIAN WORLD'. WHERE DOES YOUR LOVE AND OBSESSION FOR PLANTS STEM FROM?

I visited Bali many times in my 20s and fell in love with the incredible nature and tropical plants. As a child in urban Taipei, I felt deprived of nature as so many city people do. When I first moved to London, I lived in a flat surrounded by bricks giving not-so-spectacular views and blocking what little sun London provides. With this in mind, I chose my house in South East London because of its wonderful light and views well beyond my neighbours' walls. Recalling my inspiring trips to Bali,I started my collection of tropical plants and the rest is history.

HOW HAVE YOU LEARNED TO KEEP YOUR PLANTS SO BEAUTIFULLY HEALTHY? WHAT ARE YOUR TOP TIPS WHEN IT COMES TO PLANT CARE?

Many of my followers on Instagram ask this question. I think the number one tip I can give is to find plants that suit the climate, space and any particular quirks of the living situation they're in. The right plant for the right place is key. For instance, London, which is very northerly and has limited light, would not normally be suitable for plants that thrive in the desert. I am extremely fortunate to have a large skylight in my home allowing my plants, which I've carefully chosen after much experimentation, to thrive in this particular environment. In the darkest weeks of winter, I turn on cool, white lightbulbs, which sit above the plants and help them get through the long, dark days.

HOW WELL DOES LA LA THE CAT CO-EXIST WITH YOUR PLANTS?

We rescued La La from a carpark when she was nine years' old. It was so easy to fall in love with her as she has a real connection with humans and is very affectionate. Strangely, La La has never shown interest in or touched any of the plants, but this is an ongoing discussion on Instagram as so many people struggle to keep their cats away from plants. La La is part of my life and part of my jungle, and I include her in many of my Instagram posts. She's become the subject of many enquiries, so we've given her an Instagram account of her own: @LaLaSongCat.

TELL US ABOUT YOUR AESTHETIC AND HOW THIS RELATES TO YOUR INDOOR JUNGLE?

As a vintage art and objects dealer, I frequent many flea markets and other sources of art and objects throughout Europe. I am always on the lookout for vintage rattan plant stands, small stools and ceramic cache pots for displaying my plants. I like to have a large mix of pots,

Jamie's pothos vine is one of his more famous plants on Instagram. Using small hooks, the vine has been trained up the wall, creating a dramatic living, ever-growing feature.

WHY DO YOU THINK IT'S IMPORTANT FOR PEOPLE TO BRING GREENERY INTO THEIR SPACES?

There are so many reasons why I love indoor plants. As urban dwellers, we live, commute and work with such limited access to the green space that nature affords others. Having greenery in your living space provides a connection to the earth and nature, while also being your daily reminder of the importance of protecting our environment. From a décor standpoint, indoor plants are an affordable choice to fill your living space. You can create many points of interest at home by mixing pots of various sizes and colours, both contemporary and vintage. Visual interest can be created by hanging plants from the ceiling and by using plant stands of varying heights. Also, caring for plants can be quite therapeutic. Some people like to meditate, and I choose to care for my plants for the same beneficial effects.

YOU HAVE AN ENVIABLE COLLECTION OF GORGEOUS INDOOR PLANTS. HOW DO YOU GO ABOUT CHOOSING PLANTS TO ADD TO YOUR COLLECTION?

My top criterias for choosing plants are colour, finding plants that don't require too much sun and seeking out the unique or unusual, rather than the trendy. Leaves that are not green but otherwise colourful always pique my interest. I started acquiring plants about six years ago and can now count nearly 100 in my living space.

HANGING PLANTS FEATURE HEAVILY IN YOUR SPACE, WHAT ARE SOME OF YOUR TIPS FOR CREATING AND CARING FOR A HANGING JUNGLE?

I buy large, lightweight fruit bowls and make my own hanging planters. Plants that tolerate a little standing water can be watered directly from the top of the ladder. I keep the others wrapped in a wicker basket and cut a hole in the bottom. This means I have to take them down from their perches in order to water and then drain them completely before re-hanging. It's a lot of work but well worth it.

WHERE ARE SOME OF YOUR FAVOURITE PLACES TO GET INSPIRATION FOR YOUR INDOOR JUNGLE?

I frequent the East London plant shops and the wholesale flower market. The variety of plants available is all the inspiration I need to add to my collection.

jamie's jungle **THE JUNGLES**

style note

• While the Pothos wall creates an impressive feature all on its own, we love how Jamie has played with scale and paired it with a more delicate potted Moth Orchid (*Phalaenopsis orchid*).

> Hanging plants do require a bit of extra effort when it comes to watering, but the visual effect they have on a space makes it worth it.

CREATIVITY

Eva Luursema, metalworker + her two cats, Sonar and Phurba

GROWN WILD

AMSTERDAM, NETHERLANDS

Plants played an important role in Eva Luursema's upbringing in rural Netherlands, which explains a lot when you take a peek inside the plant-filled Amsterdam apartment she has lived in for the past 18 years, and currently shares with her two cats, Sonar and Phurba. Her wild and natural plant style means letting the plants do their thing without rules or regulations. The west-facing side of the apartment gets the most light and so this is where most of them reside. "I tend to fill every inch of space near my major light source with plant babies, cuttings and seeding experiments. Success with such experiments is never guaranteed but the ones that do work are all the more rewarding." Since space is at a premium, Eva is constantly gifting plants to friends to make room for more, and so the cycle of a plant addict continues!

THE JUNGLES

Poetic is the word that comes to mind when you see inside Eva's apartment. The artist lets her plants grow organically which creates a very authentic and homely feel for her space.

TELL US ABOUT YOURSELF …

I grew up in a small village surrounded by farms and fields. We had
a big garden and I especially remember chickens, an enormous
(or so it seemed) elderberry tree and the small apple tree I was given
as a birth-gift. Later on, we moved to a small city. After I left home,
I moved around a little before settling in Amsterdam. I've lived here
now for about 25 years, 18 of which I've spent in my current place,
which I share with my two cats, Sonar and Phurba.

Creativity plays a big role in my life – drawing, making collages,
creating objects with bits and pieces I find outside (from rocks and
rusty bike parts to dead insects and dried flowers, to mention just a
few…). In the last few years I have started working with metal, which is
a very versatile material. It opens up many new possibilities, especially
when used in combination with other materials.

HOW DOES YOUR LOVE OF PLANTS PLAY INTO YOUR CREATIVE PRACTICE AS A METALWORKER?

At the moment, I do all-round metal work. I work with my partner
who has his own business in Hertogenbosch (in the southern part of
the Netherlands). Creativity comes in handy in this job. There's great
variation in the things we do, from fixing and adjusting things to
making furniture and objects, along with larger constructions, such as
stairs, gates and facades, which again are quite different from the tiny
jewellery stands we recently made. I leave the really heavy stuff to my
partner, as he also does classic blacksmithing jobs. This seems very
different from the 'green' side of my life, but for my personal creative
projects I do take inspiration from plants and flowers – I love their
shapes and structures.

WHY IS IT SO IMPORTANT FOR YOU TO LIVE SURROUNDED BY GREENERY?

My love of plants stems from where I grew up as a small child,
surrounded by green and flowers. Also, my father was always busy
with houseplants and collecting seeds outdoors. A few of the plants
in my place used to be his. One of them is part of a cactus (someone
once mentioned it was a Night-blooming cereus. The cactus was
huge, so I only took a cutting), which I saw blooming for the first time
in my life on my windowsill! That being said, I don't have any particular
favourites, I just love to see them all thrive. Well, maybe I do have a soft
spot for the ones I've grown myself! All the greenery is very important
to me because it brings me a sense of peace, growth and life without
being loud. A sort of silence and calm, but with a persistent 'being'.

It's been proven that plants improve productivity, so what better accompaniment to Eva's work desk than an unsual mix of Alocasias, Spider plants and Aloe vera.

"My love of plants stems from where I grew up ... surrounded by green and flowers."

HOW DO YOU ADAPT YOUR PLANT CARE TO GET THEM THROUGH THE COLDER MONTHS?

In winter, when there is less light and it gets cold outside, I do not change their care habits. There is one plant – a self-grown pomegranate – that loses its leaves in winter and grows new ones each spring. This is one of my plants that needs an altogether more tropical home; it's not doing very well ...

HOW WOULD YOU DESCRIBE YOUR DESIGN AESTHETIC?

My aesthetic doesn't have much to do with 'design'; instead, it's rather organic and there is no great plan behind it. Inspiration comes from anywhere green, including hortuses (enclosed gardens), parks, garden shows on TV, from anywhere, really. Oh, and plant-filled windows as I make my way across town.

I am very picky as far as colours and placing objects are concerned (metal workers work in millimetres), so I know very well what I do or do not like, but the coming together of everything just sort of 'happens' as I go along. Just as I leave my plants to do their thing (while providing for them the best that I can).

Eva's cats Sonar and Phurba enjoy the jungle-like vibes of their plant-filled home.

creativity grown wild   **THE JUNGLES**

THE CONCRETE

The Barbican Conservatory

JUNGLE

LONDON, UK

Lush is a serious understatement when describing this extraordinary jungle. Established above the main theatre within the Brutalist concrete structure of London's Barbican Centre, this is one hell of a green oasis. But it is perhaps this juxtaposition with the harsh concrete that really makes this space special. It is the second largest conservatory in London, after Kew Gardens, with a steel and glass roof covering an astonishing 2137 square metres (23000 square feet). What was originally designed by the Barbican's architects Chamberlin, Powell and Bon to hide the massive fly tower that services the theatre below, has become an incredible collection of plants encompassing over 2000 species from around the world. The space is split into two main houses: the larger room is home to tropical species, such as Date palms, Monsteras and coffee plants; while the smaller room is called the arid house, which unsurprisingly houses an incredible collection of Cacti and Succulents. Planted between 1980 and 1981 and officially opening in 1984, public access to this incredible green space, while free, is limited. Unless that is, you're lucky enough to attend one of the lavish events held within the space or get the opportunity to shoot for a particular indoor plant book!

THE JUNGLES

The Barbican Conservatory is a huge space to fill so the gardeners had to think big. Enormous Monsteras, Banana trees and Yukka palms all form part of this incredible indoor jungle.

THE JUNGLES the concrete jungle

style note

• The large flat paddle-like leaves of the Fiddle leaf fig juxtapose beautifully with the spiky fan-esque leaves of the Mediterranean Dwarf palm behind it. The eye dances through the different shapes and textures.

> Giant Monsteras cling to walls, Devil's ivy cascades down from above and Maidenhair ferns arch delicately over the rails. This eclectic mix of foliage creates texture and depth.

POTHOS

Jono Fleming, interior designer + stylist

PALACE

SYDNEY, AUSTRALIA

The apartment of interior stylist Jono Fleming sits within a unique complex in Sydney's Waterloo. Thoughtfully designed around an inner garden, the block feels like an oasis in the middle of the city. Although living by himself now, Jono previously shared his apartment with friends. When his last flatmate moved out they took their large Fiddle leaf fig with them which was swiftly replaced with a totem of Pothos. "I missed having something green in the corner," says Jono. Soft, natural light and a regular watering schedule meant that within a few short months the easy-care Pothos was absolutely thriving. As the vines grew Jono began stringing it up the wall and then along another; who knows where this prolific plant will end up? In addition to the indoor greenery, an undercover balcony extends the living space out and is filled to the brim with fabulous foliage. Without much of a view to speak of Jono was intent on creating his own, and the plants in this space provide a decidedly lush outlook from both the living room and bedrooms.

HOW DO YOUR PLANTS IMPACT THE FEEL OF YOUR SPACE AND WHY IS IT SO IMPORTANT FOR YOU TO LIVE SURROUNDED BY GREENERY?

Living in an apartment in inner-city Sydney means I don't have much of a view. I always knew I wanted to green up my interior and balcony to create a little garden oasis. It's my view from home.

WHERE DOES YOUR LOVE OF PLANTS COME FROM?

I never considered myself a green thumb, but as I've continued to grow as a stylist I've realised how important plants can be to keeping an environment feeling lived in with natural elements.

HOW HAVE YOU LEARNED TO CARE FOR YOUR PLANT BABIES?

Out of necessity, really. I realised that if I wanted to keep my view outside looking beautiful, I had to look after my plants. I chose plants that don't need much attention or maintenance, but still look lush and green.

AS A STYLIST WHAT ARE SOME OF YOUR FAVOURITE WAYS TO INCORPORATE GREENERY INTO A SPACE?

Big, oversized greenery makes such an impact in an interior space. I don't think there is a need to always fill every corner with items, but, if in doubt, greenery is always a sure win. I love putting a big branch in a vase and using that as a centrepiece, too. It saves money from buying flowers, while still making a big statement.

HOW WOULD YOU DESCRIBE YOUR PLANT STYLE?

I think my style is a mix of whatever grows! I am now in the hands of my vine. It's a bit *Little Shop of Horrors* and the plant is definitely in control. But I love the randomness and overgrown nature the ivy has given my apartment. It's something really special.

WHEN IT COMES TO VESSELS, HOW DO YOU GO ABOUT SOURCING HOMES FOR YOUR PLANTS?

I like to find vessels that are simple, but with some character. Homemade pots and planters have a story behind them and pots with slight textures give a simple object so much personality.

WHERE ARE SOME OF THE PLACES YOU FIND INSPIRATION? ARE THERE ANY AMAZING PLANT-FILLED SPACES YOU'VE VISITED?

I recently travelled to Marrakech and I was blown away by the lush, tropical spaces hidden behind dirt roads and busy, dusty streets.

Jono has created the perfect outdoor room on his lush plant-filled balcony. Elephant ear alocasia, a variety of Succulents and stripy *Calathea* provide a wonderful oasis and green outlook from his living room and bedroom.

style notes

• Many plants will grow just as well in water as they do in soil. Glass vessels allow you to experiences the intricate root system as well as the plant's foliage.

A WELL-

Leah Hudson-Smith, interior stylist, Wally,
Sonny + Benson the dog

DESIGNED LIFE

Sick of inflexible rentals that restricted the way she wanted to live, interior architect Leah Hudson-Smith went searching for an alternative. "As a designer, I like to experiment with ideas through making and moving things around to see what fits," says Leah. The result is an incredible warehouse in Melbourne's inner north, which Leah and her partner Wally have transformed into the perfect living and working space.

'Mini houses', constructed by the pair on a very limited budget, sit within the larger warehouse and allow them to constantly adapt the interior as they please. The flexibility to shift the way their home functions from season to season is both 'practical and a bit of fun'. What Leah and Wally have created for themselves and their growing family (son Sonny arrived a week after our shoot) is a unique home packed full of plants, travel trinkets, textiles and handmade furniture experiments.

The scale of the warehouse has allowed for the inclusion of many large sculptural plants. Mature Monstera, *Schefflera* and *Dracaena* create drama in the minimal interior and sit beautifully alongside smaller *Strelitzia*, Ferns and *Ficus*. "I'd rather live exactly how I want to, instead of being held to some crappy landlord that won't fix the plumbing!", says Leah.

THE JUNGLES

Leah has a more minimalist approach to design and indoor planting. White walls and light-hued timbers reign supreme and provide the perfect backdrop for their collection of *Dracaena*, *Rhipsalis*, Monstera and *Spathiphyllum*.

YOU LIVE IN AN AMAZING WAREHOUSE SPACE. HOW DO THE PLANTS IMPACT THE DYNAMIC OF YOUR HOME?

The plants in our warehouse are my medicine, and taking care of them is a relaxing ritual that encourages me to slow down from my (often too busy) life. While they also serve as a functional air-cleaning service, for me, the benefit of living with plants is directly connected to a sense of wellbeing. Living and working in the city, I have always tried to escape to nature in some capacity every other weekend. But with the long hours of my work and the stress it inevitably brings, I realised this wasn't enough, so I started introducing indoor plants to my home as a remedy, and have never looked back!

HOW DO YOU CHOOSE YOUR PLANTS?

The plants I select are always about colour and form. I certainly don't claim to be a plant nerd and I couldn't tell you their scientific names, but together they create a composition that works for me and my home aesthetic. I try to balance height with density, and I am always moving the plants around the warehouse in order to capture different light conditions and stimulate new growth.

WHERE DOES YOUR FASCINATION WITH PLANTS COME FROM? WERE THEY PART OF YOUR CHILDHOOD?

My mum has a green thumb and we explored some great gardens together when I was young. My dad has always been into the Australian bush and we went on many epic camping trips in the Outback when I was growing up. I have always been encouraged by them to respect and explore nature, to listen closely and notice the details.

WHAT WAS THE INSPIRATION BEHIND BUILDING 'MINI HOUSES' IN YOUR RENTED SPACE?

I was tired of renting places that were inflexible. I found the traditional rental house to be too restrictive for the way I wanted to live, so I started looking for an alternative. The warehouse is perfect; I can chop and change things whenever I want, and the space is transformed dramatically with the seasons as we use it quite differently come winter. The 'mini houses' are both very practical and a bit of fun. Why build a regular room when you don't live in a regular house?

One of Leah's self-built 'mini houses' sits within the walls of their rented warehouse home. This design feature, along with their plant collection, adds warmth and cosiness to the otherwise industrial space.

AS AN INTERIOR DESIGNER DO YOU ENCOURAGE YOUR CLIENTS TO USE PLANTS?

Yes, as often as possible. I'm a huge believer in integrating natural forms within our built environment. However, it is certainly project specific; if a client has no intention of taking care of plants, then there is no point in supplying them. You need to understand each individual and how they maintain or operate in their space from day to day, not to mention access to natural light and ventilation. It's always depressing to see a shopping mall with a bunch of sad-looking plants in a dimly lit corner, which someone has clearly just drawn on the floorplan without really thinking about how it's going to work.

YOU'RE ALSO A WOODWORKER CREATING BEAUTIFUL PIECES FOR YOUR BRAND BY.PONO. HOW DO YOU JUGGLE THIS WITH YOUR INTERIOR DESIGN JOB?

I'm a busy lady! I started making things with timber and experimenting with woodwork in the evenings and on the weekends for fun. I haven't made much lately though, as I was pregnant with little Sonny and that definitely slowed me down for the first time in years. I'm kind of liking the new pace, so the woodwork is on hold for now!

The glossy green leaves of a Birds nest fern perfectly complement the neutral tones of Leah's home.

MANUAL OF SAINT-GERMAIN-DES-PRES BY

PHILIP JODIDIO

THE JAPANESE

REINVENTED

style notes

• Graphic monochrome artwork and some thoughtfully placed greenery creates a striking yet minimal vignette. Plants do a great job of balancing and softening the bolder features of a space.

• Plants pair beautifully with organic elements and neutral tones, such a these woven baskets and hats.

PLANT

Janneke Luursema, photographer

STILL LIFE

If beautiful photos of plants on Instagram are your jam, then you would almost certainly know the work of Netherlands-based photographer Janneke Luursema. Better known as @still_____ to her 100,000 plus Instagram followers, she is a keen observer of the connection between people and nature, and her serene images capture the beauty of living surrounded by plants. With plants filling the living room, kitchen and bedrooms of the two-storey Amsterdam apartment she shares with her husband, three kids and two cats, it truly is an indoor oasis.

It was an increasing craving for nature that inspired this urbanite to start bringing plants into her home, but it also coincided with a decision to stop having babies. From her favourite Monstera to a variegated *Ficus elastica*, Janneke's plants aren't merely subject matter or inspiration for her work, but they are in themselves, "living works of art that are always changing," says Janneke. Happy, thriving plants give the space a sense of calm, which Janneke finds both relaxing and comforting. While her collection is extensive, there are always some special plants on the lust list. "Even just dreaming about expanding my little jungle makes me so happy!" So what's next? Tracking down the elusive variegated Monstera, of course!

THE JUNGLES

YOUR LOVE OF PLANTS IS SOMETHING YOU'VE COME TO
RELATIVELY RECENTLY, AND YOU'VE GONE FROM SELF-CONFESSED
BLACK THUMB TO PLANT MAMA IN A PRETTY SHORT SPACE OF
TIME. WHAT CHANGED FOR YOU?

Living in the city, I started to crave nature more and more. Collecting
houseplants was a relief for me, as they soothe the soul. I do my best
to keep them healthy and happy, but it's a matter of trial and error.
Some thrive in my home, while some are unhappy and sometimes even
die. It's mostly a matter of balancing light and water.

WHAT EFFECT DO PLANTS HAVE ON YOUR SPACE AND THE WAY IN
WHICH YOU AND YOUR FAMILY ENJOY IT?

Plants create a relaxed and comforting atmosphere and they're so
enjoyable to be around. They are living works of art, which are always
changing and interesting to look at. I think being surrounded by
houseplants is a healthy thing, but only if you can manage to give
them the care they need. You don't want it become a chore. Looking
at unhappy plants can be interesting from an artistic point of view,
but it can also give rise to stressful feelings.

PLANTS FEATURE HEAVILY IN YOUR PHOTOGRAPHY WORK. HOW DO
THEY INSPIRE YOU AND WHAT DO YOU LOVE ABOUT SHOOTING THEM?

In general, nature and the circle of life inspires my work. Plants are
works of art themselves and I never get bored of their shapes, colours
and textures. With the changing of the seasons and, therefore, the
changing of the light, it's a different scene every day. Life itself is
a miracle – amazing and beautiful.

HOW DOES YOUR STYLE RELATE TO YOUR INDOOR JUNGLE?

I like to collect a variety of colours, textures and shapes, but I also
ensure that the plants are suitable for the conditions in my home.
I started with a huge collection of vintage pots that I had collected
over the years from thrift shops. But lately I tend to use simple
terracotta pots, to create a more calming atmosphere and leave
maximum room for the plants themselves to attract the eye.

CAN YOU TELL US ABOUT SOME OF YOUR FAVOURITE INDOOR PLANTS?

I like the Monstera, a lot. Mine hasn't matured yet, and every time
a new leaf unfurls I'm hoping it will have fenestrations, but that hasn't
happened yet. Exciting times ahead! Also the variegated *Ficus elastica*
is a feast for the eyes. I love the fairy-like Asparagus fern, but also the
Bird's-nest fern and the Staghorn fern and the Blue star fern …

The perfect gentle light that makes Janneke's photographs so special also keeps her plant collection in tip-top condition. Here a Fiddle leaf fig arches towards the window while plant stands, shelves and benchtops are covered in various Begonias, Cacti, Calatheas, Mother in law's tongues and Bromeliads.

> **"I tend to use simple terracotta pots, to create a more calming atmosphere."**

ARE THERE ANY PLANTS THAT YOU'D LOVE TO ADD TO YOUR COLLECTION?

Yes. I would love to add a variegated Monstera to my collection, but they aren't easy to get your hands on over here. I haven't even seen one in real life yet, only on Instagram! Also a Zig-zag cactus is really missing in my collection, in my opinion. And a Lady's slipper orchid, but not a purple–pink one. Even just dreaming about expanding my jungle makes me so happy!

WHAT ARE YOUR KEY STYLING TIPS FOR PEOPLE WANTING TO INTRODUCE PLANTS INTO THEIR SPACE?

You have to really make sure the conditions in your home match the needs of the plants you bring in, so research before you buy. I like to group plants because they seem to like that (it's something to do with humidity), and I think they enhance each other's beauty. Combine different sizes, colours, textures, shapes and variegated foliage to create interesting vignettes to look at.

WHERE DO YOU FIND INSPIRATION FOR BOTH YOUR DESIGN AND ART PRACTICE AND YOUR INDOOR JUNGLE?

Art is a huge inspiration for me. Artists I admire include Van Gogh, Vermeer and Hopper. I also find inspiration in my houseplants and garden, botanical gardens, woods, beaches and mountains. People and nature. The changing seasons. What the light does. The small things. The ordinary.

Naturally aged terracotta mixed
with other pots of neutral tones
and textures provide an unfussy
and honest base that allows
Janneke's plants to do the talking.

plant still life   **THE JUNGLES**

HORTICULTURAL

Thomas Denning, horticulturalist

HAVEN

<u>MELBOURNE, AUSTRALIA</u>

Childhood memories of days spent tending to his grandparents' veggie patch surrounded by the beauty of the Tasmanian wilderness inspired the now city-dwelling Thomas to pursue a career in horticulture. On moving into his modern, light-filled apartment in Melbourne's Northcote he sought permission from the landlord to install wall-mounted shelving in the bedroom and living spaces, which he promptly began adorning with plants. These lush ledges house an array of both trailing and upright foliage, and it is the arrangement of such diverse leaf shapes, colours and textures that make them such a striking feature in the interior. Safe to say almost every surface of the rented apartment now sports some form of greenery and the space is all the better for it. Amassing such an extensive collection – up to 150 plants at any given time – has taken years, but Thomas's collection is constantly evolving. "Over the years I have both bought and given away plants, which has helped me to focus on a particular species or genus that I really enjoy having in the house."

YOU'RE A HORTICULTURALIST AND AVID PLANT LOVER. WHERE DID YOUR LOVE OF PLANTS COME FROM?

My love of plants has been ticking away in the background for most of my life. The green thumb gene runs deep on both sides of my family, but it wasn't until later in life that I decided to pursue horticulture as a career. Some of my most vivid memories from childhood are from spending time in the veggie patch with my grandparents or helping my parents construct their latest garden project.

WHY IS IT SO IMPORTANT TO YOU TO LIVE SURROUNDED BY GREENERY?

Being surrounded by greenery has become such an important aspect of my life, I can't imagine living in a space without some kind of botanical feature. The routine of watering and caring for my plants at home is quite calming and meditative, providing a bit of an escape from inner-city living.

YOU'VE GOT AN ENVIABLE COLLECTION OF WEIRD AND WONDERFUL PLANTS. TELL US ABOUT SOME OF YOUR MOST PRECIOUS PLANT BABIES.

It's always so hard to pick a favourite, but my obsession with some of the weird and wonderful botanical species was sparked by *Dioscorea elephantipes*. It's native to South Africa and has the most bizarre appearance and growth habit. From there I entered a rabbit-hole obsession with Caudiciforms and Epiphytic cacti.

YOU LIVE IN A SMALL INNER-CITY APARTMENT. WHAT ARE YOUR TOP TIPS FOR STYLING AND DISPLAYING PLANTS WITH LIMITED SPACE?

Small-space living does come with its limitations, but incorporating greenery doesn't have to be one of them. My collection usually sits between 120 and 150 plants at a time, with a few of them going to new homes through trades or presents to friends.

You don't need a huge amount of plants to make a big impact in a small space; sometimes a few statement plants can completely change the aesthetic of a room, so it's really up to you how you choose to 'jungle up' your home. I love using plants en masse to create visual interest in my house. Shelving and furniture pieces that have multiple uses work best for me. That way you can visually change things up as you need without restriction. Contrasting leaf shapes and plant-growth habits really grab my attention, so don't be afraid to pair odd things together.

My number one tip would be to select the right plants for your home. It's worth spending the time investigating the environmental factors in your space. Watch how the light moves throughout the year and how your heating and cooling impacts your plants.

Controlled chaos is how Thomas describes his design aesthetic. Here, his collection of beautiful handmade ceramics adorn shelves housing a mix of trailing foliage. Graphic air plants peek out between the potted plants.

IN ADDITION TO YOUR AMAZING PLANT COLLECTION YOU HAVE AMASSED SOME GORGEOUS CERAMIC VESSELS TO HOUSE THEM. HOW DO YOU GO ABOUT SOURCING THEM AND WHO ARE SOME OF YOUR FAVOURITE MAKERS?

We are really lucky to have a thriving and vibrant ceramic community in Melbourne, but it has also developed throughout Australia and the world. I find quite a few artists through Instagram or word of mouth. Makers can really express and represent their work well on Instagram, reaching a global audience from wherever they are based. There are so many talented makers out there at the moment, it's almost impossible to choose, but some of my favourites would be Wingnut & Co., It's a Public Holiday, James Lemon, Anchor Ceramics, Dot & Co., Sophie Moran, A Question of Eagles, Leaf and Thread and Arcadia Scott.

HOW WOULD YOU DESCRIBE YOUR DESIGN AESTHETIC?

Controlled chaos would be the best way to describe it. I have slight hoarding tendencies, which can be hard to keep in check at times. A lot of my vintage pieces have come from eBay or local antique furniture stores (Grandfather's Axe in Northcote, Melbourne, is a treasure trove), so it's a bit of a mish-mash of art, vintage furniture and greenery. I tend to be drawn to more neutral/natural tones, which pair well with my plants.

YOUR PLANT SHELFIES ARE SOME OF THE BEST ON INSTAGRAM. HAVE YOU GOT ANY TIPS FOR DRESSING SHELVES WITH PLANTS (THE TYPES OF PLANTS THAT WORK BEST, PLANT PAIRINGS, COMPLEMENTARY VESSELS)?

That is so kind of you to say! Cascading plants and shelving are a match made in heaven. It's always good to integrate personal objects and some greenery to give life to a space. Contrasting foliage is key. I find the diversity of Hoyas and epiphytic Cacti, such as *Rhipsalis*, really visually amazing, plus they're easy to care for. They both range from big, dramatic growth habits to smaller, softer forms.

YOU'VE VISITED SOME INCREDIBLE GREENHOUSES AND PLANT-FILLED SPACES ON YOUR TRAVELS. WHAT ARE SOME OF YOUR FAVOURITES AND WHY?

Walking into the greenhouses at Kew Gardens, London, was one of those jaw-dropping moments. After reading and lusting over the gardens for so many years, it was amazing to finally experience them in the flesh. There is so much that goes on behind the scenes to keep the gardens looking at their best, so working there is definitely on the dream job list.

A large potted Chinese money plant, an Elkhorn fern kokedama and a vase full of Marimo moss balls make up a small part of Thomas's extensive and unusual plant collection.

COLLECTOR'S

Anno Leon, DJ and photographer

CORNER

SYDNEY, AUSTRALIA

A self-described avid collector, Anno Leon revels in the "thrill of finding unique and interesting things, whether it's digging through music, exploring vintage shops or visiting local nurseries to find that elusive plant!" The Newtown terrace he shares with flatmates and two very chilled cats, Mali and Miko, is a product of his plant treasure hunting. His collection has sprawled throughout the home as well as taking over the balcony, patio and backyard. If there's natural light, it's a potential spot for plants! A skylight in the bathroom provides the perfect light for some hanging greenery that thrives in the humid room. "It's a pretty nice view from the shower too," says Anno. His bedroom is the exception, as this is where he propagates and grows his prized plants under grow lights.

Anno's latest plant obsessions are Aroids and Begonias, which add some seriously graphic foliage to his plant gang. Handmade ceramics also feature heavily in the space and his ability to pair them with their perfect plant pal is a real gift. The happy and healthy jungle that Anno has amassed is so much more than just a collection of plants. The process of tending to them and "simply pausing to appreciate the subtle changes in their growth every day, is a great way to stay present. Having a green space to work and live in helps maintain a sense of calm."

Anno mixes handmade
ceramics, aged terracotta and
rattan baskets to house his
stunning plant collection.

WHY IS IT SO IMPORTANT FOR YOU TO LIVE SURROUNDED BY GREENERY?

Being surrounded by greenery is a wonderful feeling. Having the freedom to arrange and combine different shapes, patterns and textures and knowing they can evolve over time into a beautiful living picture really gets me excited. I'm an early riser and my morning ritual involves a brew of strong coffee and a wander around the garden with my watering can and snips. It's a great way to set myself up for the day and makes me feel grounded. Simply pausing to appreciate the subtle changes in growth every day is a great way to stay present, and having a green space to work and live in helps maintain a sense of calm. I often listen to mixtapes – usually a mix of mellow grooves, jazz and ambient electronica – or podcasts while gardening. I'm currently working on a series of mixtapes called Sanctuary, a blend of ambient music and nature samples.

WHERE DOES YOUR FASCINATION WITH PLANTS COME FROM? WERE THEY PART OF YOUR CHILDHOOD?

I grew up living with my uncle and auntie in the western suburbs of Sydney. They enjoyed growing edibles, such as Asian greens, herbs and tropical fruits. I have fond memories of helping in the garden, sowing seeds, harvesting vegetables for traditional recipes and learning how to cook them. In recent years, my interest in collecting plants was sparked through a special person who was in my life. She had a beautiful light-filled apartment by the ocean with lush greenery, and it was where I spent a lot of time being in love. That's when my fascination for Begonias began and I developed a desire to learn more.

YOU CLEARLY LOVE BEGONIAS. WHAT MAKES THEM SO SPECIAL? DO YOU HAVE ANY PARTICULAR FAVOURITES IN YOUR COLLECTION?

They really are! I find them intriguing with their alluring textures, shapes and patterns. It is such a diverse genus, including shrubs, cane stems and rhizomatous varieties, to name a few. Some of my favourites are *Begonia venosa* and *Begonia peltata* for their unique shapes, felt-like texture and grey foliage. Both originate from South America. *Begonia goegoensis* is a fascinating rhizomatous species with a metallic bronze hue, delicate veins and red underside, native to Sumatra. Then, of course, there's the one that started this little journey, *Begonia maculata*, an angel wing cane variety with dramatic silver spots and deep-red undersides.

care notes

Some of Anno's top progagating tips:

• If propagating in water, I find smaller vessels are better, as they encourage the plant to release hormones, which speeds up root development. Place in a bright spot away from direct sun. When it's time to pot up, I prefer small pots to allow the soil to dry faster between watering. I usually use a mix of premium potting soil, perlite and vermiculite.

• For stem and node cuttings, I find sphagnum moss and vermiculite work really well. I place cuttings in a tub, drill a few holes for ventilation and place under grow lights. The humidity really helps the roots to develop!

HAVE YOU EVER STUDIED PLANTS ACADEMICALLY OR HAVE YOU JUST LEARNED FROM EXPERIENCE?

I've never studied plants academically, so I've learned mostly from experience, experimenting and reading lots of books. I enjoy researching species that capture my imagination and I try to memorise their botanical names and care requirements. Working at The Plant Society has presented some insights into plant care and maintenance, and this has helped me to better understand how plants respond in different light situations.

YOU TAKE BEAUTIFUL PHOTOS OF YOUR PLANTS. WHAT DO YOU LOVE MOST ABOUT PHOTOGRAPHING PLANTS? AND WHAT ELSE DO YOU LOVE TO CAPTURE THROUGH YOUR LENS?

Thank you! I enjoy the process of arranging different types of foliage with interesting patterns and forms. When out and about, I'm drawn to landscapes with greenery. I love exploring different neighbourhoods and admiring other people's gardens. Overgrown landscapes, abandoned places and scenes that can often change with different light situations are also interesting to capture, especially on film.

YOU'RE AN AVID PROPAGATOR. HOW DOES IT ALLOW YOU TO CONNECT WITH OTHER PLANT LOVERS?

I love experimenting with different propagation techniques. It's a nice way to grow your collection without spending too much money and I find it more rewarding than buying established plants. Instagram has been a great way to connect with other plant lovers, exchange knowledge and share ideas. I've learned a few propagation techniques this way and have traded many cuttings with some lovely people. I also love sharing my plants with friends and I'm always happy to snip a few cuttings or give away extras when they visit.

WHAT ARE YOU FAVOURITE WAYS TO STYLE PLANTS?

I like to group my outdoor plants so they eventually grow into each other, which can often create interesting layers and pattern combinations. I love the character of aged terracotta but also favour beautiful handmade planters for my indoor plants. Rattan baskets are great for lush foliage plants and add a classic feel to any space.

collector's corner   **THE JUNGLES**

style notes

• Smaller potted plants jazz up Anno's bathroom, providing a decidedly lush view from the shower.

• Bathrooms can be small, but by utilising existing surfaces, such as the top of the cistern, you'll find plenty of spots for plants.

> An enviable collection of perfectly patterned Begonias mix with the green foliage plants in Anno's covered courtyard.

URBAN

Nick Simonyi, event manager

GREEN OASIS

MELBOURNE, AUSTRALIA

The rented Flemington house of plant enthusiast Nick, his partner Pete and their jack russell Henry is also home to a beautiful collection of indoor greenery. Moving from a smaller apartment in Melbourne's South Yarra to better accommodate Henry, the extra room has also allowed for the expansion of Nick's indoor jungle. The incredible light in the bedroom means many plants fill the room but, as is often the way they have come to inhabit nearly every room of the house. Adorning shelving, mantles, plant stands and furniture, the foliage brings life to every surface. Originally hailing from Brisbane, Nick describes his aesthetic as 'a little eclectic and Melbourne-centric'. His space is furnished with a beautifully edited collection of furniture and decorative elements, many of which have been created by local makers and creative friends. His collection of handmade ceramics is enviable and they provide beautiful homes to many of his plants.

Nick's tip for creating the
perfect plant shelfie ...
"I love a good ceramic and
a good trinket, and often
sit them among my plants
for added intrigue."

THE JUNGLES

WHERE HAS YOUR LOVE OF PLANTS COME FROM?

Initially, I think it had a lot to do with the hours and hours I spent in my grandmother's garden in Brisbane as a child. She had the most beautiful garden, and she'd spend six or seven hours a day out there. Even when she wasn't gardening, you'd find her sitting out under a massive eucalyptus tree enjoying a cup of tea. I spent a lot of time out there with her as she taught me about the plants she grew and tending to her garden through the seasons. I then lived with one of my closest friends in Brisbane who had a sizeable indoor plant collection. We also worked together, and on our days off we'd frequent a couple of indoor plant nurseries and tend to a joint collection of plants (though they were mostly hers) – she definitely ignited my love for indoor greenery.

HOW HAVE YOU LEARNED TO KEEP THEM SO BEAUTIFULLY HEALTHY?

Trial and error, 100 per cent. I've killed more than my fair share of indoor plants; it's all about learning and adapting your environment and plants to find what makes each individual plant happy. My top tips are to consider the natural state of your plants (how do they grow in the wild; what sort of conditions do they thrive in?), paying attention to their needs and any changes in their foliage, and ensuring that they get the right amount of light.

WHY IS IT SO IMPORTANT TO YOU TO LIVE SURROUNDED BY GREENERY?

For me, surrounding myself with indoor plants and taking the time to care for them makes me slow down, plus it gives me a bit of a break. I love the 30 minutes I spend once or twice a week without my phone, not checking emails and just focusing on my plants. It's calming and I find it a great way to practise mindfulness. It helps that they look good, too!

YOU HAVE AN ENVIABLE COLLECTION OF GORGEOUS INDOOR PLANTS. HOW DO YOU GO ABOUT CHOOSING YOUR PLANTS?

I'm not overly picky – I just choose what I like and what grabs me when browsing in plant stores. Of late I've made a more conscious effort to go for quality over quantity, and to tend to some more special plants. I've recently added a few Aroids to my collection that I love, and I am currently enjoying plants with interesting and unusual foliage.

THE JUNGLES   urban green oasis

Nick brings a shelf to life with hardy Hoyas and a Syngonium sitting next to an enviable Chinese money plant. All look the business in organically shaped ceramic homes.

PLANT SHELFIES FEATURE QUITE HEAVILY IN YOUR INSTAGRAM FEED. WHAT ARE SOME OF YOUR SECRETS FOR DECKING OUT SHELVES WITH GREENERY?

I have to credit the same housemate from Brisbane for my love of a plant shelfie – she introduced me to them. It's just such a great way to welcome plants into any space without having them everywhere (at least, that's the idea). I don't think there's any secret to decking out a good plant shelf – just happy plants (again, ensuring they're getting enough light) and some added styling elements. I love a good ceramic and a good trinket, and often sit them among my plants for added intrigue.

HOW DO YOU GO ABOUT SOURCING THE CERAMIC VESSELS THAT HOUSE MANY OF YOUR PLANTS? WHO ARE SOME OF YOUR FAVOURITE MAKERS?

We're so lucky in Melbourne! There are so many talented ceramicists and artists here who make some beautiful ceramic planters, vessels and artworks. I love a good ceramic samples and seconds sale, but so many plant stores in Melbourne also stock locally made ceramics. My favourite ceramicists are Laura Veleff of Leaf and Thread (@leafandthread), James Lemon (@jameslemon) and a friend of mine who has taken up pottery and now lives in Canberra. She's sent me a few absolutely beautiful planters and ceramics, and they're that much more special when a good friend has put so much care into sculpting them.

WHERE ARE SOME OF YOUR FAVOURITE PLACES TO GET INSPIRATION FOR YOUR INDOOR JUNGLE?

Instagram, of course. There's also just so much to see in Melbourne with so many stores, restaurants and cafes decked out in beautiful greenery. I worked at the Higher Ground cafe when I first moved here and eventually started tending to the indoor plants in the venue – that was great! Then there's the boutique plant stores and nurseries in Melbourne: The Plant Society, Plant by Packwood, Greener House, Fitzroy Nursery ... I could go on forever. They always provide great inspiration for my own plants at home.

Nick with one of his precious plant babies, an Alocasia black velvet. It's thriving thanks to the bright, indirect light it receives in his living space.

style notes

• Nick has collected handmade ceramics from many of Melbourne's talented makers. He loves a good sample sale and also scours local plant stores to find the perfect homes for his plants.

• Plants on a shelf are complemented by other objects and trinkets. Botanical wares, such as these secateurs, look right at home.

> *Monstera siltepecana* cuttings growing well in a propagation vase. Larger potted plants line the walls in the background creating a decidedly lush living space.

PLANT MAMA

Jenna Holmes, creative director of Plant Mama

HEADQUARTERS

MELBOURNE, AUSTRALIA

Smack bang in the heart of Melbourne's Collingwood, a two-storey 1890's Victorian home has been transformed into the seriously lush HQ of Plant Mama, Jenna Holmes. Full of character and greenery, Jenna has been given *carte blanche* from a generous landlord to create her ideal urban oasis. Having grown up in country Queensland with 'a consistent connection to nature and the outdoors', moving to inner-city Melbourne was quite a shock to the system. Filling her space with indoor plants became a necessity. "My little plant retreat made the bustling vibe outside my door bearable," but for Jenna, it also led to a major career change from PE teacher to plant stylist.

The new digs have allowed Jenna to bring her plant aesthetic to the public, as the building also functions as an event space for pop-ups, photoshoots and other activities. It's an opportunity to showcase her green style and hopefully inspire others to create their very own plant-filled interiors. The available lighting dictates the plants in each room – the more light, the more plants. Jenna has made particularly good use of the light-filled staircase leading to the private areas of the dwelling. Here, a massive Fiddle leaf fig sits alongside other *Ficus*, Philodendrons and plenty of Pothos, emulating the overgrown 'disorganised jungles' she tends to favour.

Mirrors are a wonderful
way to up the lush factor,
instantly multiplying
the foliage.

More is definitely more when it comes to the plants at Plant Mama HQ. Jenna describes her plant style as "organised chaos with a splash of 70's design. The more chaotic the better."

TELL US ABOUT THE ROLE PLANTS PLAY IN YOUR LIFE, FROM LIVING IN A PLANT-FILLED HOME TO CREATING URBAN JUNGLES FOR OTHERS.

Plants have played a revolutionary role in my life, but it all comes down to the effect they have had on my mood and my environment. I grew up in country Queensland, meaning we always had space, loads of greenery and a consistent connection to nature and the outdoors. When I moved to inner-city Melbourne, I struggled with the absence of that connection, so bringing plants indoors and incorporating them into my space really changed the way I felt in my home. As I built my first indoor jungle, my creativity and styling work came alive and it felt right. I was teaching High School Physical Education at the time and fortunately there wasn't anyone else providing a 'jungle-building' service, so I threw myself into it. I then realised that others were craving the same connection that I was, and I was very happy to help create their jungles for them.

YOU COME FROM A PROUD FAMILY OF PLANT LOVERS AND AVID GARDENERS. HOW HAS THAT INFLUENCED YOUR LOVE OF PLANTS AND YOUR CURRENT WORK WITH PLANT MAMA?

It has been the number one influence – Plant Mama is an ode to the plant mamas who have come before me. My mother and grandmothers were all avid plant lovers, and they incorporated plants into every aspect of their homes, both inside and outside. When I looked at how they styled their plants I realised we were all very similar. Having people before me trial and error all the happenings with plants has given me the shortcut answers to ensure happy and healthy jungles for all my clients. The knowledge that they passed on is invaluable, and I still call my mum and ask her questions (to which she knows all the answers). Most clients have a story about a parent or grandparent in the garden with them, and I am so thrilled to re-open that connection to plants for them.

WHY DO YOU THINK PEOPLE SHOULD LIVE SURROUNDED BY GREENERY?

I think you can argue that even a small amount of greenery can relax the soul, and there has been study after study to support this. I think it is just a gentle reminder of the other living things surviving in this world besides us, and another living thing that requires considerable care and attention in order to survive.

An incredibly lush corner of the studio is created by a mix of large floor plants, full trailing specimens and some of the healthiest Boston ferns going around.

"Plants have played a revolutionary role in my life."

WHAT ARE SOME OF YOUR KEY STYLING TIPS FOR PEOPLE WANTING TO INTRODUCE PLANTS INTO THEIR SPACES?

It's all about layers and heights. Things need to be built in a layered way: add a plant, step back and have a look and then add another. The step back is the most important part of the job.

WHEN IT COMES TO POTTING PLANTS, WHAT ARE SOME OF YOUR FAVOURITE VESSELS AND WHERE DO YOU SOURCE THEM?

I source my pots from a range of places! In order to create a different vibe for each project, you need to shake up the vessels as the plant varieties tend to be somewhat consistent. I visit op shops, pot shops and random nurseries, and I buy a lot online as well. The pots have the biggest impact on the design of a space, so their selection is an important part of the process.

YOU LOVE TO TRAVEL. WHERE ARE SOME OF YOUR FAVOURITE PLACES TO VISIT FOR 'PLANT-SPIRATION'?

Travel is why I work. It is hands-down my favourite passion, even more so than plants. I LOVE Europe's plant game, especially in Italy and Greece – all the overgrown balcony gardens, Cacti, terracotta pots, and even more so the owners of the gardens; they are such cuties and essentially other plant mamas. I always come back from an overseas trip filled with ideas for my next jungle. I like to think of my travel as creative research!

Jenna sitting pretty
among the greenery in
her inner-city Melbourne
Plant Mama HQ.

A STYLIST'S

Lucinda Constable, owner of The Table New York

STUDIO

<u>NEW YORK, USA</u>

Living and working within a three-block radius is a rarity in New York, but such is the dream situation for stylist and owner of The Table New York, Lucinda Constable. The Australian creative lives by herself in her sun-dappled apartment and shares her studio with a bunch of creative friends (plus a few life-sized stuffed animals). The plants in her studio were inherited when she moved in and brought much-needed life to the space from day one. She believes they play a big part in creating what is an incredibly supportive community, and they certainly give the space a distinctive lush vibe. At home, large statement plants including a massive Fiddle leaf fig and Monstera drink up the natural light that pours into the living room of her south-facing apartment. "Natural light is my number one must have and thankfully both my apartment and studio have an abundance of it."

Hanging plants are trained across the ceiling to create a lush canopy of leaves in Lucinda's studio.

HOW LONG HAVE YOU BEEN LIVING IN NEW YORK AND WHEN DID YOU SET UP YOUR BUSINESS THE TABLE NEW YORK?

I have been in New York almost seven years now. It's hard to believe! I set up my company three years ago, and it all snowballed quite fast – I have the Australian grapevine to thank for that!

DO PLANTS PLAY A ROLE IN YOUR STYLING WORK?

Plants play a huge role in my styling work. I always try to rent full-sized planted varieties for events to completely transform the space. It's an instant mood changer. I consult regularly with a wellness-focused company, bringing amenity spaces to large office buildings in Manhattan, which are usually devoid of natural light, have low ceilings and 80s carpets. Plants are integral and have become our signature, especially the hanging Pothos, which does well in low light.

WHAT DID YOU LOOK FOR WHEN SEARCHING FOR YOUR APARTMENT AND STUDIO SPACE?

Real estate in New York is one of those eternal struggles, always sacrificing one thing for something else, and so on. No place is perfect! Natural light is my number one must have, however, and thankfully both my apartment and studio have an abundance of it, being south and west facing, respectively.

HOW HAVE PLANTS CHANGED THE DYNAMIC OF BOTH SPACES?

Plants immediately make a room feel more lived in and homely. They evoke a sense of tranquillity, which is necessary in a home or work environment. I can't imagine living without plants; it would feel so sterile.

WHAT ARE SOME OF YOUR KEY STYLING TIPS FOR PEOPLE WANTING TO INTRODUCE PLANTS INTO THEIR SPACES?

Start small and build on it. I have known people to binge-buy twenty or so plants in one go, without learning what works in the space. Plants are like children – they need to be nurtured! I suggest starting out with more hearty and stable plant varieties, such as a Monstera – a firm interior favourite!

style notes

• A massive Fiddle leaf
fig soaks up the indirect
light streaming through the
nearby window and makes
a beautiful statement in
the living area.

• Lucinda has selected
a relatively neutral palette
for her interiors, which really
allows her large-leafed green
plants to pop. Moroccan
rugs and woven baskets
add charm to this crisp,
clean space.

HOW WOULD YOU DESCRIBE YOUR PLANT STYLE?

My personal style is sculptural and graphic, across the board. All the plants in my home sit alone and have their own thing going on. Each one has a lot of personality! They work well with the rest of my graphic decor and colourful art collection. It makes me so happy! The studio is more lush and jungly, which works well there, but it would not translate to my living space.

WHERE ARE SOME OF THE PLACES YOU FIND INSPIRATION?

I love finding inspiration at the Brooklyn Botanic Garden. It's nestled in Prospect Park and has a wonderful greenhouse, as well as beautiful cherry blossoms in spring. It's a bit more wild than the manicured New York Botanic Garden, but both are lovely. Other favourites include the Jardín Etnobotánico de Oaxaca in Mexico and undoubtedly the Jardin Majorelle in Marrakech. I love it when you unexpectedly find a lush oasis in the middle of barren land, and Marrakech is perfect for this. Some of the best spots include the Beldi Country Club, El Fenn and the aptly named Le Jardin. Obviously getting out and about is the best way to discover new spots, but 90 per cent of my inspiration unfortunately comes from trawling Instagram and interiors' blogs.

Floor to ceiling windows in her New York studio create the ideal light conditions for plants.

a stylist's studio   THE JUNGLES

About the authors

Lauren Camilleri and Sophia Kaplan are the plant nerds behind Australian-based plant business Leaf Supply. Believing life is better surrounded by all things green, Lauren and Sophia are on a mission to spread their love and knowledge of plant care and styling.

Lauren is a magazine art director and indoor plant specialist who owns online plant and design store Domus Botanica, and Sophia is the plant and floral stylist of her namesake business Sophia Kaplan Plants & Flowers, and founder of the blog The Secret Garden.

As their business has grown, so too have their families, Sophia is mum to son Raf and Lauren to daughter Frankie. The Leaf Supply team has also grown to include fabulous plant lovers, Beth, Sarah and Adi.

Indoor Jungle is the pair's second book and follows on from *Leaf Supply*, a guide to keeping happy houseplants.

thank you

THE OPPORTUNITY TO MAKE ONE BOOK IS AWESOME but to be asked to come back and make another is something we are eternally grateful for. A big thank you to our publisher Paul McNally at Smith Street Books for your trust and encouragement. Even though we are yet to meet in person, it was a pleasure to work again with our editor Lucy Heaver; we so appreciate your expertise in helping to guide us and shape these pages.

To the amazing photographers who helped capture our vision all over the world: Luisa Brimble (Sydney + Melbourne), Anna Batchelor (London), Lillie Thompson (Melbourne), Lynden Foss (Byron Bay), Jess Nash (New York), Janneke Luursema (Amsterdam) and Aidan Rolls (Berlin). Thank you for taking our brief and creating these most magical images. This book would be nothing without your photographs.

We were welcomed with endless hospitality into the homes and workspaces of so many lovely plant people. Thank you for your passion for plants and for being so willing to share it with others. Your thoughtful responses to our interview questions truly demonstrate that plant people really are the best type of people.

To all the people who let us pick their brains about plant-filled spaces in their faraway homes: Lukas, Talitha, Mikarla, Lara, Lucinda and Anna, we appreciate your time and insider knowledge.

Last but not least, a big heartfelt thank you to our growing families ...

SOPHIA Thank you to Mum, Janice, and Dad, Lewis, for always giving me the space and unending love and support to work on this book along with everything else. Thank you to Aunt Rosie who contributed fabulously to the plant profiles, to my sister, Olivia, for endless babysitting, and partner Mike and baby Raf for being the best fellas to have by my side. And, finally, thank you to Lauren for jumping at these opportunities and bringing your incredible aesthetic to all our projects, while juggling pregnancy and a newborn, which is no small feat, that's for sure.

LAUREN Growing and birthing a baby while making a book at the same time is quite the daunting scenario, but thanks to the incredible support from my mum and dad, business partner Sophia and, of course, my husband Anthony, *Indoor Jungle* was born around the same time as baby Frankie.

PUBLISHED IN 2019 BY SMITH STREET BOOKS
MELBOURNE | AUSTRALIA
SMITHSTREETBOOKS.COM

ISBN: 978-1-925811-25-4

PUBLISHER: PAUL MCNALLY
SENIOR EDITOR: LUCY HEAVER, TUSK STUDIO
DESIGN CONCEPT + LAYOUT: LAUREN CAMILLERI
PHOTOGRAPHY: LUISA BRIMBLE, PAGES 2, 6, 10, 15, 16, 29, 35, 44,
45, 49, 52–53, 55, 56, 57, 61, 62, 65, 69, 74–75, 77, 78, 79, 80–81, 82,
86, 96, 104, 106, 107, 114, 117, 118, 120, 121, 143-151, 179-185, 205–239,
248, 254; ANNA BATCHELOR, PAGES 20, 25, 38, 46, 50, 51, 102,
108, 125-131, 153–161, 171–177; AIDAN ROLLS, PAGES 37, 110–111, 113,
133–141; JANNEKE LUURSEMA, PAGES 4–5, 23, 32–33, 36, 43, 60,
94, 163–169, 197–203; JESSICA NASH, PAGES 70, 241–247; LAUREN
CAMILLERI, PAGES 58-59, 66–67, 68, 85, 90–91; LILLIE THOMPSON,
PAGES 9, 40, 47, 187–195; LYNDEN FOSS, PAGES 18–19, 72, 73, 84,
89, 99

PRINTED & BOUND IN CHINA BY C&C OFFSET PRINTING CO., LTD.

BOOK 107

10 9 8 7 6 5 4 3 2 1